The Vale of]

Its Picturesque Peeps and Legendary Lore

John Salkeld Bland,

Editor: F. H. M. Parker

Alpha Editions

This edition published in 2024

ISBN : 9789362090560

Design and Setting By
Alpha Editions
www.alphaedis.com
Email - info@alphaedis.com

Contents

INTRODUCTION.

THE river Lyvennet rises on the northern side of the range of hills stretching eastwards across Westmorland from Shap Fells. It runs through the parishes of Crosby Ravensworth and Morland, receives the tributary stream of the Leith, and falls into the Eden near Temple Sowerby. The distance from its source to its outfall is less than ten miles measured in a straight line; but the little valley is full of varied interest, to which each age has contributed a share. Half way down the stream, and out on the west, lies Reagill, and in it, Wyebourne; and Wyebourne was the home of John Salkeld Bland, who, nearly fifty years ago, compiled this manuscript history of "The Vale of Lyvennet."

John Bland's grandfather was a yeoman farming his own land at Reagill. He had a family of two sons, Thomas and William, between whom he divided it; Thomas, who was an artist and sculptor of no mean ability, remaining at Reagill, while William established himself at Wyebourne, a mile away, married, and also had two children; one being John Bland himself, the other a daughter, now Mrs. Dufton, to whom the thanks of this Society are due for use of her brother's manuscript, and for her kindness in supplying information about the family.

John Bland was only six months old when he lost his mother, from whom, perhaps, he inherited a constitutional delicacy from which he always suffered. He was educated at the well-known school at Reagill, and afterwards at Croft House, Brampton. Early in life he began to show a gift for drawing, but he never received lessons; his aptitude, like that of his uncle, was purely a natural one.

He also studied botany, geology and chemistry. Before he was twenty-two he had made a geological map of the district; this came before the notice of some of the leading authorities of the day, and received high praise from them; it is interesting, therefore, as it affords us proof of the high standard of merit reached by his work. He afterwards went over to America for a time; an expedition comparatively rare in those days. During the summer of 1866 he made studies from nature of about a hundred wild flowers, painted in water colours, and had just finished mounting them before his death. For his weakness of health had shown itself in attacks of pneumonia when he took cold; finally consumption set in, and he died on January 4th, 1867, aged twenty-seven years.

But the work in which we are most interested is his manuscript "The Vale of Lyvennet." The book consists of ninety-one pages about 12 by 10 inches, filled with drawings and plans, of which there are about two hundred, large and small; with a written description of each. Infinite pains have been spent upon it. He has taken each object of local interest in turn, recorded minutely what is known about it, and accompanied it with at least one drawing. The work has not been quite completed, as the last three pages, and pages 79 (a beautiful half-page drawing of Flass House), and 82, lack text; there are a few blanks left for measurements, and several spaces for pictures. It is, of course, the pictures that give the book its unique character, for they make everything a reality to the reader. The drawings themselves are beautiful; but even apart from them, a better account of the valley could hardly have been made, either in material or arrangement. And it is not unworthy to add that the text is written in the most delicate penmanship, almost as finely executed as the drawings themselves.

But his studies were not confined to antiquities or art, nor his reputation to his native valley. Mention has already been made of his geological work. The map was submitted to the Manchester Geological Society at a meeting on December 30th, 1862, with a paper entitled:—"On the Carboniferous Rocks in the neighbourhood of Shap and Crosby Ravensworth: a section of that series which lies on the northern and eastern extremities of the Lake District." He also submitted a section from Wasdale Crag to the valley of the Eden near Appleby—distance about ten miles; which, with the paper, was printed in the Society's *Transactions*, vol. iv., p. 44.

Mr. Bland was unable to be present, and the paper was read by Mr. E. W. Binney, F.R.S. Mr. Binney, who was one of the most eminent geologists of the day, afterwards made the following remarks:—"I became acquainted with Mr. Bland last year, in going over that district to look over some property. He showed me this map, and it occurred to me that I had not seen any map of a limestone district so well worked out by a local man. Mr. Bland has devoted many years to the examination of the becks and gills of his district, and has formed this section. I think the paper a very valuable one, because it shows how the limestone begins to be separated by coal measures."

Mr. Joseph Dickinson, H.M. Inspector of Mines, President of the Society, added:—"I could have wished for the map to be published as well. I do not think we could hand over our funds for a better purpose." But the expense was a serious matter, and the map, now preserved at Reagill, does not appear ever to have been published. The paper is written in a much more matured style than the present work, possibly because he is writing of matters that can be ascertained with greater certainty; he expresses himself in the manner of one who has a complete mastery of his subject.

As to the sources of his information, Mrs. Dufton says that his account of the manorial disputes was derived from a collection of old parchments in the possession of Mr. Salkeld of Meaburn Hill, his great-uncle; representative of a family which had been resident in the locality since the reign of Elizabeth. To attack sixteenth century documents for information must have required a great deal of enthusiasm, especially in one with such a love of outdoor life; for these documents are dreary things, and, as Mrs. Dufton observes, they were very hard to read. Another instance of the thoroughness of his work is shown in the fact that he reproduces the heading of one of these in the old writing, an undertaking by no means easy; and an excellent reproduction it is.

He had evidently read a great deal, and had gone carefully through most books that describe his neighbourhood, and he collected and stored up what was related to him by his friends. His industry was extraordinary, and he is said never to have wasted a moment of time.

He probably owed much to Canon Weston, then vicar of Crosby Ravensworth, who took a kindly interest in his work, and used to invite him to the vicarage when he had visitors interested in science or archæology. Among those whom he met were Canon Simpson, first President of the local Archæological Society, who was then incumbent of Shap; and Professor Harkness, who once filled the Chair of Geology at Queen's College, Cork. He was also appreciated and helped at Lowther, where he saw the paintings by Lady Mary Lowther (wife of the famous "Sir Jammy," the first Earl) some of which he copied; while no doubt he learned a great deal from his uncle, Thomas Bland.

The latter, a man of varied talents, also deserves some notice here. He was famous for his Italian garden at Reagill, which he laid out and decorated with statues and oil paintings in the alcoves, all his own work; he was an excellent artist in black and white, and reputed to be a musical composer of merit.

His nephew tells us of his sculpture commemorating Charles the Second's halt at the head of the Lyvennet, and of the stone he set up to mark the place where the forefathers of the famous Joseph Addison had their home in days gone by. But there is another work which can be seen by everyone; a pedestal and pillar surmounted by a figure of Britannia, executed by him, and erected at his expense, on the hill facing Shap Wells Hotel, to commemorate the accession of Queen Victoria. It was placed there in 1842; the railway close by was opened in December, 1846; so it stands within the view of all.

Mr. Bland did not attempt to immortalise himself by putting his own name upon it; it is a pity that persons visiting it have not been equally modest; for the pedestal, which bears bas-reliefs and an inscription, has been defaced by idlers for more than half a century, as their dated scratchings show.

He also celebrated this event each year by a large entertainment. This is mentioned by Whellan in his *History of Cumberland and Westmorland*, written in 1860, who says:—"A festival of a somewhat unique character is held here (at Reagill) annually, on the anniversary of Her Majesty's accession, on the grounds of Mr. Bland, which are richly ornamented with pictures, statuary, etc. A band of music is engaged for the occasion, and the days amusements are interspersed with lectures, addresses, music, dancing, and other recreations." The gathering was actually held on the Friday nearest to the anniversary; on some occasions as many as 1,400 guests were present.

No memoir of Thomas Bland would be complete without some account of the wonderful garden that he planned and made. John Bland has preserved one view of it in its old splendour; it is reproduced at the end of this book. The wall on the right of the entrance was known as "The Local Gallery," as paintings of local scenes, Shap Abbey, Lowther, Brougham and others, were mounted in alcoves there. Beyond, near the angle of the wall, was the "Shakespeare Gallery." Facing the entrance stands Sir Walter Scott; below three bas-reliefs, that on the right of the spectator representing Rob Roy, that in the middle Bois-Guilbert fighting on horseback, striking Athelstan down; the third, Prince Charlie.

On the left of the entrance is a terrace with a statue of Music, holding a lute, emblematic of the Lyvennet; there are also statues of Addison, Burns, and Hugh Miller the geologist; for Thomas Bland, like his nephew, was interested in geology. This terrace stretches away to the left; against it, and facing the lower lawns beyond was a building for the musicians. The whole garden was lavishly decorated with paintings and sculptures; the last of the former were removed from the walls about three years ago. It seems almost incredible that one man should have accomplished so much work; but he had a marvellous facility for rapid work and simple execution. He could finish his work very finely, but seldom did so.

A description of the gardens, and the statues in particular is contained in Anthony Whitehead's *Westmorland Legends and other Poems*. It would have been pleasant to say something of Mr. Whitehead, whose memories are so closely connected with the work of the Blands; but it is a delicate matter to write of a man in his lifetime; and he is still living, and bearing his ninety-one years very lightly. Two of his stanzas are quoted in this book, to illustrate the tale of Crosby Hall.

Thomas Bland worked at art for its own sake, cared nothing for fame, and would have hated notoriety. He had at least one excellent chance of becoming known to London art circles, for David Cox (the younger), who had seen some of his drawings, was interested, and wished to introduce him to his friends. He gave Mr. Bland several of his own water-colour paintings, and some correspondence passed between them; but the introduction fell through. He had, of course, many visitors, some of whom came to see him only from idle curiosity. These he could not endure. For their benefit he had a large oleograph of Garibaldi set up in his studio. If they fell into the trap, and admired it, they were summarily dealt with, for he could be brusque to those whom he did not care about. The Garden Beautiful was free to all; but he would not sacrifice time or convenience to a bore—least of all, an admiring bore.

There is one story told of a trick which was played upon him: about 1855 he went to Kendal to hear a lecture on electricity. He was sceptical of the marvellous powers claimed for it, and refused to believe that it would be impossible for him to let go the handles of the battery when the current was turned on. Having the courage of his disbelief, he went upon the platform to try, and unsuspectingly put his top hat between his knees. Then the operator turned the current on strong, and it was only after that top hat was fairly flattened in his struggles that he was released, amid the roars of the audience; whereupon he fled from the room and back to Reagill, a wiser man—with a ruined hat.

He seems to have been credited with a certain amount of eccentricity, though this may have been due to a commonplace reading of unusual gifts and vigorous originality; but it is certainly the case that he was highly esteemed as a man of warm heart and kindly disposition, which attracted all with whom he came in contact; and in his own neighbourhood his death was greatly deplored. He died on September 18th, 1865, in his sixty-seventh year, unmarried.

But John Bland's work, good as it is, has an additional value, because there was at the time no systematic effort in this field of research. The Cumberland and Westmorland Antiquarian Society held its inaugural meeting on September 11th, 1866, only four months before he died, and for some six years not much was done. Thus he was the first to plan the important stone circle at Gunnerskeld. This, like its neighbour at Oddendale, belongs to a class, rare in Britain, which consists of concentric rings of stone. Mr. C. W. Dymond, F.S.A., in publishing a plan of Gunnerskeld circle, says:—"So far as my researches have extended, no plan of this megalithic group has ever been published, nor, save in a local guide book, have I ever seen it mentioned." The book contains a drawing, a ground plan and a description of each of these remains.

But he never lapses into dulness. Indeed, he pokes quiet fun at the antiquary pure and simple. Certain earthworks, he says, have been supposed by some antiquaries to be a maze; a dilemma in which antiquarians are sometimes found. Writing of Crosby Park, he has a gentle thrust at those who deal of venison and vert, and ancient deer parks and forests:—"These things," he says, "are past and gone, except to the dreaming poet and the prosing antiquary."

His sketches cover a wide range. He puts before us each object of which he writes; heraldry, old buildings, picturesque landscapes, down to the bracelets and rings found in Skellaw quarry. And each of these pictures is a work of art, for his was a genius that touches nothing it does not adorn. He had no mean imagination; there is a vivid picture of a man on horseback, rider and beast recoiling in terror before the vision of the Headless Horseman of Gaythorn Plains, which is galloping across their track in the moonlight. He has a humorous picture of a "Ghost seen by Bet Whistle"—a dead pollard tree, which makes a most menacing apparition, though probably the ingenuity of the artist has something to do with it. And over the first page, majestic in flight, soars the Roman eagle.

It has been possible to reproduce only a limited number of his drawings: in making a selection (no easy task), some preference has been given to those which represent objects no longer existing.

In dealing with the text, variations have been made as seldom as possible, and then where the author might have wished an alteration, in accordance with later discoveries. Thus, the account of the settlement at Langdales has been curtailed, as its great mystery, a bank running from the pre-Roman village across the Roman Way, has been explained by the recent discovery that the bank is modern. Part of the account of Harberwain is left out, as he takes *Har*, on the authority of a distinguished local antiquary, to be a man's name; and reasons accordingly. It really means *high*. Some of the quotations from Ossian are left out, as, though appropriately introduced, they divert attention from Mr. Bland's own work. The chapter on the history of Crosby Church, compiled from Charleton's *History of Whitby Abbey*, is omitted, as a recent account of the church has been published; while in the present book certain limits of size had to be observed. Incomplete sentences, where details of measurements are wanting, have generally been deleted.

This brief memoir attempts nothing more than a record of the life and work of John Salkeld Bland. If he should be forgotten, we should be the poorer for the loss; and yet his work was done so unobtrusively that a studied appreciation seems out of place. The publication of his book may cause his name to be connected in local literature with that of the Lyvennet. Perhaps this is the most fitting memorial for him—to be remembered as the chronicler of the valley he loved so well.

WICKER STREET.

The Roman Road connecting the Stations at Borough Bridge and Kirkby Thore.

THE earliest historic record respecting the North of England was made by Tacitus, from whose works we learn that the Roman armies led by Agricola first advanced into this district and conquered the inhabitants then known as the Western Brigantes in the year A.D. 79, in the reign of the Emperor Vespasian.

The base of Agricola's operations was Chester, (Deva), the station occupied by the 20th Legion; with these he advanced northwards by the modern towns of Manchester, Preston and Overborough, and up the vale of Lune to Borough Bridge, at each place forming a station and connecting them by roads cut through the forests; the last station he placed in the only pass by which Westmorland could be conveniently entered from the south-west.[1] From Borough Bridge the road had gone nearly direct to Kirkby Thore, traversing the whole length of the vale of Lyvennet. Many antiquarians supposed it went to Brougham, but the name Wicker Street applied to an extensive hill on the west side of Crosby—a name significant of a Roman way—led to examination a few years ago and a road was found traceable from near Black Dub to Dale Banks, a distance of more than two miles, indisputably in the direction of Kirkby Thore: it is regularly formed and rounded in the middle, about thirty feet across, the ground being generally hard and dry; no trace of paved work is to be found.

The march of Agricola's army is said to have been straight as the track of a sunbeam, and his roads are generally considered to be carried in a direct line surmounting every obstruction. However this may have been in an open country, it is more reasonable to suppose that in a district like this they would overcome a difficult ascent by deviating to the right or left. In leaving Borough Bridge they have crossed the Lune twice, considerably to the right, in preference to going straight over the steep hills and numerous ravines of Loups Fell, which would have been almost impossible; then again, where are the first traces of the road, instead of ascending the steep cliff of the scar near Bousfield How, they have gone to the west, ascending and so coming by easier gradients to the top of Wicker Street. This is the most commanding point overlooking the vale of Lyvennet, and no doubt, as its name implies, it was an important point to the invading Roman armies, Wicker Street according to some authorities meaning "the gateway of the pass." It was from this point probably that Agricola's army first beheld our lovely valley; for he, after establishing a stronghold at the gorge of the mountain pass at Borough

Bridge would either lead or send out a party of soldiery to survey the country northwards, a district abounding in forests and fastnesses in which roamed the fierce and revengeful Britons; their scouts would of course avoid the craggy heights of Orton Scar, and following up the course of the stream from the north be led to ascend by the way along which the road was afterwards laid out: though we may reasonably allow that all the low districts were at that time densely wooded, yet it is highly probable that on the high lands were extensive openings clear of wood, or perhaps here and there patches of brushwood; such the character of the soil and its general void of wood at the present time leads us to imagine; the only brush now to be seen is on the top of the hill and known as Wicker Street Thorn, which, like the Shap Thorn and Johnny Hall Trees is a guide mark for many miles round. Here by the side of the road is a square oblong enclosure of earth and stones which, after the construction of the road perhaps served as a *mons exploratorum* by which, and others such, the garrison at Borough Bridge could be warned of the approach of the enemy. The road from this point descends and crosses the Blea Beck; an embankment has been raised on each side and brought near together; quantities of huge boulders have been used to bank it up and probably form a culvert. From here it crosses Slack Randy, passing near some entrenchments and curious stone circles called Yow Locks and descends Long Dale. In this field on the brow of the hill above Dale Banks is what antiquarians affirm to be a British village; it presents earthworks covering three or four acres of ground: these consist of irregular squares, circles, &c., formed of earth thrown up to the height of from one to three feet.[2]

Continuing the course of the road, it is traceable to the bottom of the hill, where it has crossed Odindale beck, after which all further traces have been obliterated by enclosures and the plough; the direction however is straight for Kirkby Thore, crossing the Lyvennet near Dairy Bridge, where there is an ancient paved wath, then past Lofterns and over Castriggs in King's Meaburn township, across the Eden about two hundred yards above the present bridge at Bolton, where there are remains of an abutment, as of a bridge, with mason-work and grouting now overgrown with brushwood; thence in the direction of Kirkby Thore joining the more important road known as Watling Street from Bowes in Yorkshire. No remains of decided Roman character have ever been found in connection with this road, but this is accounted for by the fact that no settlement was made in the valley, it being but a thoroughfare along which passed and repassed the Roman legions employed in the somewhat vain attempt to subjugate the wild Caledonians. It is possible this road or track was previously used, but of this we have no proof, but from that time up to the making of the present road over Shap Fell it was used as the great highway between the southern parts of England and Scotland.

EARTHWORKS.

THE SITES OF ANCIENT BRITISH VILLAGES.

THE most important monuments left by the ancient Britons who inhabited this country previous to the Roman invasion are the several remains of villages. Cæsar, in describing what the Britons call a town, says:—"It is a tract of woody country surrounded by a vallum and a ditch for the security of themselves and cattle against the incursions of their enemies." Strabo confirms this, and says further:—"That within the inclosures formed of felled trees they build houses for themselves and hovels for their cattle: these buildings are slight, and not designed for long duration." The vallum is expressed in Welsh by *caer* or *dinas*, the same with the Gaelic *dun*. Diodorus Siculus and Strabo tell us that the houses of the Gauls were wretched cottages, being constructed with poles and wattled work in the form of a circle with lofty tapering or pointed roof, and Cæsar also says that the houses of the Britons were similar. These it is true were of south Britain, but it is reasonable to infer that with little alteration those of the northern inhabitants would be similar. Some authors suppose the present Welsh pigsty to represent the form of the ancient British house. This is a circular building with a conical roof, and having a large circular enclosure attached.

In the district under consideration there are remains of earthworks which may be considered of this character. They generally consist of ridges of earth and stones varying in height from one to three feet, forming irregular squares, circles, passages, &c., covering a greater or less area of ground. In five of these are to be found small circular enclosures generally six yards in diameter, with a gap or opening on one side; each of the other larger enclosures have also an entrance and in some places a sort of street or passage communicates. The most extensive and distinct are the remains of Long Dale, which are skirted by the Roman road: in the middle part of these are seven or eight of the small circles. Another though much smaller is on Wickerslack Moor: this has five small circles, with two or three irregular squares and a large circle; a large area is also enclosed on the high side which is not cut up by any earthworks. In two of the small circles was found a rude pavement formed of large slabs of sandstone rudely laid down and fit together with smaller boulders of granite, &c., but no limestone; these stones bear evident marks of having been exposed to fire. The ground chosen for these enclosures without exception are upon the hard limestone rock, covered by a very thin layer of earth; this with the loose rock has been bared off and used to form the earthworks. They are also generally at a considerable distance from water.

Yow Locks, another of these villages, is on the open moor called Slack Randy; here only one or two small circles can be traced; but the ridges are very marked, many of them being formed of large boulders rolled together. These are very plentiful near; there are two peculiar oval enclosures formed solely by large boulders, the longer diameter of each being nine yards. Another village may be seen in a field near Gilts; though very irregular, yet it affords traces of eight or ten of the small circles.

How Arcles, a little above Wood Foot affords a large circle, but only one or two of the small ones; these may have been obliterated by the plough. Bellmouth, probably a corruption of Bermont, is another between Reagill and Sleagill; part of this is quarried away, and about twenty years ago a human skeleton was found behind one of the outer earthworks. Another on Wickerslack Moor has only one small circle attached to a larger one, and enclosed by a large irregular square. The new road cuts through it, and the plough will soon obliterate all trace of it, as it doubtless has done of many others in the now cultivated parts of the country. At Harberwain is another though in a great measure obliterated, yet still exhibits a few squares, &c.; connected with it is a rampart of earth; this seems to have been for some extraordinary defence.

Other entrenchments are still to be found more or less obliterated by the advance of agriculture; some of a strategic character which will be afterwards noticed, and others again that will forever puzzle enquiry for what purpose they were raised and by what people.

To the most ancient inhabitants many authors ascribe the origin of the various stone circles to be found in different parts of the country. There are two remarkable ones in this district, one in Gunnerskeld bottom, and another near Odindale Head. The former is situated on a level area elevated a little above the bed of the stream. It is a circle of large granite boulders eighteen in number, some of which are still standing upright seven feet high, while many have fallen one way or the other. The circle is thirty-eight yards in diameter; and within it is another formed by thirty-one stones much smaller in size and eighteen yards in diameter; within this has been apparently a mound, most of which is removed for the sake of the stones and the earth has been thrown into a heap outside; there are still some large stones left and three in the centre are situated as though they may have formed part of a cromlech. There is no record of anything having been found, and the word Gunnerskeld is of too modern a character to throw any light on the matter.

The one near Odindale Head is similar, at first sight inspires a truly Ossianic feeling. It is situated on a hill of "dark brown heath," it is formed of an outer circle of thirty stones not so large as those at Gunnerskeld, twenty-five yards in diameter, within which is another circle of twenty-one stones closely packed to each other seven yards in diameter; within this are a number of other stones irregularly laid, similar to Gunnerskeld. It was opened in presence of Rev. J. Simpson, but nothing was found excepting a small portion of black carbonaceous matter. A peculiar feature is that there is an upright stone placed outside the inner and within the outer circle on the south-east side. On the north side about seven yards distant is the remains of another circle, fourteen yards in diameter, having another within of four yards, but many of the stones have been removed.

Respecting the origin of these circles authors differ considerably, some considering them to be the temples of the Druids, within whose mystic bounds sacrificial rites were performed; while others attribute them to a later people, the Pagan Saxons, Angles or Danes.

Odindale, like Gunnerskeld, is a name significant of the latter people. Odin was the one great god of the Gothic nations, from whom they all claimed descent, and to whom, of course, their greatest honours were paid.

There are also other circles much smaller in size and each on elevated ground, one near Threaplands is formed of seven granite boulders, and is five yards in diameter; some of the stones are six feet in length. Another on Harbyrn Rigg is six yards in diameter and formed of eight stones and another outside. On Wicker Street is another formed by eleven stones five yards in diameter, and near to it is a small one of four stones, three yards in diameter. Another on Harkeld is formed by ten stones, and is six yards in diameter; in digging in this one, a few inches deep was found a stratum of charred bones. The one on Harbyrn Rigg has three stones in the centre, but no trace of ashes: some of the stones are six or seven feet long, and have all originally been placed upright. These we may also attribute to the ancient Britons, probably the monuments erected around the funeral pile of important personages whose names and fame they have failed to record, but yet, in the words of the poet, "have spoken to other years."

The Druids in their temples had generally a spring or stream of water near. This is the case with the one at Gunnerskeld, but not so with the other, unless we can associate Anna's Keld with it; which is, however, half a mile distant. This well is mentioned by Camden, who says that like Euripus of old it ebbs and flows with the tide.[3] However it may have been then, it is not the case now; but devoid of this interest its position is one of dreary grandeur, being situated in the midst of the dark brown heath. To what people we may attribute the saintly name of Anna is doubtful, but it has at some time been an important spot, from the fact that it is the source of Crook Syke, whose waters have run through the gigantic temple at Shap, now known as Carl Lofts; a temple like Avebury in the south dedicated to the dread worship of the serpent.[4] It is now almost destroyed, but it is considered to have been one of the most important monuments of antiquity in the north of England.

As Mr. Bland arouses our curiosity as to the origin of remains of this kind, it may interest readers to have a short account of the various opinions which have been expressed on the subject. These have been based mainly upon researches in Wiltshire, more particularly at Stonehenge and Avebury; and if these relics prove their founders to have possessed much knowledge and ingenuity, it can hardly have been more marvellous than that embodied in some of the theories formed about them.

The first scientific report on Stonehenge was made by Inigo Jones, at the wish of James I.; he thought it was a temple erected by the Romans, after the Tuscan order. Charleton, physician to Charles II., held that it was a monument of the Danish period. Aubrey, about the same time, attributed it to the Druids. Next came Stukeley's famous theory. Stukeley, a man of great learning, had read of the Druids, and had seen the circles; then he found a grotesque story in Pliny about an egg, miraculously produced from the saliva of serpents, and regarded as a charm by the Druids. So, he reasoned, the Druids made the circles for serpent worship; and, according to his argument, the complete temple consisted of a diagram of a snake, miles long, done in boulders, the circles being the reptile's coils! To demonstrate this, Stukeley made a plan of the Avebury remains. The result was not very convincing; essential parts of the creature's anatomy were wanting; and a snake is nothing if not continuous. But he sketched in these missing parts out of his own head, and the thing was done. Somewhat similar results were got from a hurried survey of Shap, about 1725. Such is the groundwork of the popular belief in "Druids' Circles," and yet, at the time, it was received almost as a revelation. John Wood, of Bath, about 1747, introduced the idea that the numbers of the stones corresponded to certain astronomical cycles or periods of time. Rev. Edward Duke, writing in 1846, saw in the Wiltshire remains a vast plan of the solar system as known to the ancients; the small circles at Avebury were the sun and moon at the summer solstice; the avenue of stones on either side was the northern portion of the ecliptic; Silbury Hill, a mile south, the Earth. Four miles north of Silbury,

Winterbourne Basset circle stood for the planet Venus; south of it were Mercury; Mars; Jupiter, represented by Casterly Camp, nine miles from Silbury; and Saturn by Stonehenge, sixteen miles off. The vastness of the scheme will be appreciated by saying that an equivalent of this in Westmorland would place Saturn at Tebay, Jupiter at Shap, and the Earth at Eamont Bridge; or, following the railway, the viaduct crossing the Eamont. Mr. Duke notices that all the points are in almost exact line due north and south; and that Stonehenge points directly towards the sunrise at the summer solstice. About twenty years later, a good deal was made of practically the same fact, that from the so-called Altar Stone within Stonehenge, the sun on Midsummer Day appears to rise immediately over a distant stone called the Friar's Heel; hence it is argued that Stonehenge was an observatory. This is the modern popular theory, possibly because of its simplicity. Fergusson, about 1870, published a most interesting argument that these circles were set up after the Romans left; his conclusion is not generally accepted, though his views are treated with respect. Those who think that archæology must be dull, should read his racy satire at the expense of poor Stukeley. One of his suggestions is that Long Meg, or perhaps the Grey Yauds circle, may be a memorial of King Arthur's battle in the Caledonian Forest. The best opinion is that of Mr. W. C. Lukis, who thinks that the object, in the first instance, was that of burial-places; that they were formed before the Roman invasion; while Mr. Arthur Evans assigned to Stonehenge an approximate date of 450 B.C.

ANCIENT BURYING PLACES.

THE remains next under consideration are the cairns or burial mounds. These have been very numerous on the high grounds and unenclosed moors around the source of the Lyvennet. Thirty or forty may still be found perched upon the highest peaks, or otherwise on commanding situations, others on the overhanging banks of the streams, while some have been placed without any characteristic choice of site. Some of these bear significant names or more often the name is applied to an extended area of the hill or plain on which they are found; and others there are with which no name can be connected. The word *How*, Danish—a hill, is generally significant of a mound, but is often applied to the whole, as Sill *How*, Raise *How*, Bousfield *How*, *How* Arcles, *How* Neuk and *How* Robin; on each of which are mounds. *Raise* is an older word of similar meaning, and is applied more directly to a mound, as *Raise* How on Bank Moor. This name is more common in the neighbourhood of Shap. *Pen*, of Cambro-Celtic origin, having the same meaning, is found in *Pen*hurrock. Others again bear the ordinary name of *Hill*, as Iren *Hill*, Round *Hill*, &c. Though these mounds have been raised by different people each in their day, yet they are often found to have been named or rather called *Hills* by whatever word in the language or dialect of the succeeding races expressed the same. Others again there are bearing names peculiar to themselves, as *Iren* Hill, *Sill* How, *Hollinstump*, Pen*hurrock*, Robin Hood's Grave, Lady's Mound, &c. Though they are numerous, yet many of them have been opened by the hill-breakers of the last century, or been more or less ravaged for the sake of stones, earth, &c.; for this reason it is difficult to distinguish those belonging to different ages, though it is highly probable the great majority are British.

On Gaythorn Plains—an extensive tract of comparatively level moor on the north side of Orton Scar, are two mounds 100 yards apart, respectively fourteen and [ ] yards in diameter; the larger of these, on being opened by Rev. J. Holmes, was found to contain in the centre an urn of baked clay, ornamented with rude zig-zag work on the outside; this was broken but had contained ashes; besides this the mound contained remains of five different skeletons which, from the wear of the teeth, had been of different ages; some being sharp and pointed, while others were worn quite flat. It is a remarkable fact that no teeth found in any mounds show the slightest symptoms of decay.

At the extreme edge of the Plains on the brow of a cliff overlooking Sale Bottom is another mound composed solely of stones; it is twenty-six yards in diameter, and has originally been about seven or eight feet high. It is known as Hollinstump, a corruption, as some think, of Llewellen's Tomb. Llewellen was the last of the Welsh Kings, and was beheaded about 1280 in the reign of Edward I., but it is improbable the King would trouble to send his mangled remains for interment to such a distant part. It was opened by some gainseeking hill-breakers, who say they found a large slab of sandstone, under which was a full length skeleton and a small implement—in the words of the finder:—"He seemed t'eve been buried in his cleayse wid a jack-a-legs knife in his waistcwoat pocket." Of the sandstone slab:—"They brak it up an' gat three carfull o't finest sand et iver was carried to Appleby Low Brewery." Bone dust was not then come into fashion, or else we may be certain his bones would have been sold to the crushing mill. This place is said to be haunted, the apparition being a headless horseman who dashes along at a furious yet noiseless speed. Those who have seen him describe him as having in place of a head something like a blaze of fire, and others like a backboard laid upon his shoulders—perhaps the distinguished spirit of the wronged and headless Welsh King, whose sole revenge is to dash on the midnight wind around his tomb, to the terror and dismay of each benighted wanderer.

Round Hill near Towcett, was opened by a similar class, out of which was got a sandstone slab of large size, afterwards made into a chimney-piece; under it were also found human bones. A like one existed at Flatt Neuk on Bank Moor, but is now removed; within it was a cist formed of rude stones set up edgewise, in which was the skeleton, and alongside a bronze spear-head; this cist was covered by a large sandstone slab, over which had been heaped, as in the others mentioned, earth and stones even to hundreds of cartloads in quantity; in some cases brought from a large distance.

Penhurrock, the highest point by the road leading from Crosby to Orton, was a large mound of stones, but it has been removed and broken up for road metal, with the exception of a few boulders of granite. Its diameter was about twenty yards, having in the centre a cist surrounded by an irregular circle of stones about eleven yards across; the boulders are only very small, and have been covered up in the mound. A quantity of bones was found, some of them of gigantic proportions: and what is rather curious, in a small cavity on one side were found a quantity of ashes, remains of the fire by which the bodies had been consumed. As no account was kept of the deposition of its contents, in what position the entire skeletons were found, or where the ashes of those consumed had been placed, we can form no decided opinion respecting its age; but from its mixed contents it was probably used as a burial place by different succeeding races.

On Long Scar Pike is a large mound of stones twenty yards in diameter, and eight or nine feet high. It has been opened, but no account kept. There is another on How Nook Pike, a little further south; these are the highest points in the parish of Crosby Ravensworth, and are positions truly worthy as the resting-places of some ancient chieftains or warriors, overlooking as they do the vale of Orton, the Lune and their tributary dales of Bretherdale, Langdale, Wasdale, and the vale of Birkbeck with its far-famed medicinal spa, backed by the bleak and rugged peaks of Shap Fells.

On Wicker Street, near the stone circle, is a large irregular oblong mound, twenty-four yards in length, and another at no great distance, but small and circular, on the east side of the Roman road. A more remarkable one is on a limestone cliff overhanging the Lyvennet, in Crosby Gill; it is an oval, or keel-shaped, ten yards the longer diameter, and six the less, and about seven feet high.

Robin Hood's Grave is an oblong mound, seven yards by three. It is situated at the bottom of a narrow rocky dell at the head of Crosby Gill, where the footpath from Orton to Crosby enters the woods, once the chase of Sir Lancelot Threlkeld. It is noticed by Mr. Sullivan in his "Cumberland and Westmorland," but he speaks of two heaps: this is, however, a mistake, there being only one. Of this mound he says "It was once customary for every person who went a-nutting in the wood, at the south end of which this heap is situated, to throw a stone on Robin's grave, repeating the following rhyme:—

Robin Hood, Robin Hood, here lie thy bones;
Load me with nuts as I load thee with stones."

Whoever was the original of the famous outlaw, and whether he was properly Robin of the Wood or Robin with the Hood, his name is now connected with mounds and stones innumerable in various parts of England. On Ploverigg Edge are two large stones, known as Robin Hood's Chair and Punch Bowl; in short, too much popularity has converted him, according to the view of critical investigation, into a myth. Probably the well-known rhyme of schoolboy notoriety may be in allusion also to the famed outlaw of Sherwood Forest:—

Robin a Ree, Robin a Ree, if I let thee dee
Many sticks, many steanes be heaped o' my weary beanes
If I sud set Robin a Ree to dee:

This game is usually attendant on bonfires, near which, those joining the game stand in a row; the first then takes a fiery stick, and whirling it round and round repeats the rhyme, then handing it to the next, who repeats it, and so on till the stick dies out; the unfortunate individual, in whose hand this happens, is then at the mercy of the grimy sticks and wet sods of his companions.

Not far from Robin Hood's Grave is a spring known as "King's Well," which is supposed to bear its royal title from being visited by King Henry VII.; but of this we have no more reliable proof than we have that Robin Hood's remains lie beneath the mound, which, on being opened, was found to contain only an old sheep's skull.

There are three mounds near to each other on the east bank of the stream near Gilts; they are about seven or eight yards in diameter each. None of these have been opened. Between Gilts and Lodge is one; below it are a number of parallel and other earthworks, suggesting to the mind of some antiquaries the idea of its having been a maze; a dilemma in which antiquarians are often found.

A little south of How Arcles is a mound near which are circular and square entrenchments.

Lady's Mound is near the high road over Meaburn Moor, from which it is said the Countess of Pembroke once stood and remarked that she could see from that point three of her ancient castles, namely, Brough, Appleby and Brougham.

On the east side of Morland Bank is a mound on the edge of what has once been an extensive marsh now known as Redmires. It is here worthy of remark that Morland Bank is a corruption of Mere or Mireland Bank, from *mere*, a marsh; literally meaning "the bank amongst the marsh lands." It is a tongue of high ground which has at some time been almost surrounded by marshes. These though now drained still retain the significant names of Redmires on the east side, through which runs Lyvennet, and Eelmires on the west, drained by a tributary stream. That these have been more extensive and of a more marshy character is proved by the fact that when Redmires was drained in 1863, at the depth of 4½ feet, in black marshy earth, was found part of the head and horns of a deer. The skull has been forcibly broken from the neck, while the horns have been cut round with some sharp instrument and then broken off; the four tips on the part of the horns left are also cut and broken off. The remainder of the horn, being useless, has been thrown away into the marsh, on the banks of which would have been the scene of the slaughter; whether by Briton, Roman or Saxon we know not: but it is certainly a relic of the chase when the native deer of Westmorland ranged wild and free over its forests and fells. In the same drain and about the same depth was also found a small stone ornament. It is best described as half of a large marble one inch in diameter, with the top flattened and a hole made through it about a quarter of an inch in diameter, slightly wider on one side than the other; it is of blue slate. These, by some, are called Druids' rings.

Returning again to mounds, one was removed in Reagill Croft, in which was found what was called a bronze spear-head. On Wickerslack Moor another was removed, having on the original surface a layer of black earth surrounded with boulders, but all covered up. Others of various sizes may also be seen on Ploverigg Edge, Hardendale Nab, near Murbur, Potrigg, near Starbey Field, &c., possessing no features particularly worthy of remark. Near Harberwain Plantation was formerly a circle of stones eight yards in diameter, within which had been a mound; but it is all now removed.

On Harberwain Rigg is a remarkable mound occupying a very elevated position; its diameter is fourteen yards, and surrounded by eighteen large boulders. It was carelessly opened a few years ago, and in the south-west side was found a human skeleton of gigantic proportions; but whether he had been in a cist or how laid was not noticed. Along with the bones were found portions of the horns of the red deer. The mound is called Iren Hill, doubtless a corruption. Half way between it and the stone circle was found in a cleft of the rock a bronze dagger blade, thirteen inches in length and four inches broad at the hilt. It is of very good workmanship. Whether it is coeval with the mound is doubtful; but it is a good specimen of the weapon which supplanted those of the stone age, and in the hand of the Briton opposed the advance of the Roman legions. Another relic of the same age is a small bronze celt three inches in length, which was ploughed up in a field near Blinbeck, and now in possession of Mr. Markham of Morland. Iren Hill is the only mound now left in the neighbourhood having a circle of stones round.

Orton Scar, an extensive tract of high ground, is a dreary wilderness of rocks, extending for many miles, presenting little more than the bare limestone cut up in its original formation by deep chasms into blocks of various sizes. These again are carved and worn into most fantastic shapes by the wearing power of winds and rains. The only form of vegetable life flourishing in the crevices are of the fern species, some of which are peculiarly rare in other localities. Here and there are patches of earth affording a scanty herbage of bent and moss for the few hardy mountain sheep. These rocks break off on the south-east side forming bold escarpments overlooking the vale of Orton, while on the other side they slope away in the opposite direction for a mile or more, variously broken up into rocky valleys and ravines unadorned by either bush or brake. The scenery is, of course, in the immediate neighbourhood, of a wild and dreary character; but its high situation affords a wide panoramic view of the surrounding country, bounded all round by the more or less distant mountains, even to the blue line of the Cheviots. Of archæologic interest there are a few mounds located in different parts on the high elevations; but the observing eye cannot but note that it has been more a place of refuge and safety in life to the ancient inhabitants than a resting place after death; and in such localities would we expect to find the fastnesses of the Celtic races to which they would fly when the Roman armies made their appearance through the gorge at Borough Bridge, and also the people of after ages seeking safety from the marauding Scots or Danes up to the last Border foray. Associated with the last-named times is the highest point: from which often has blazed the beacon fire signalled from other heights, and warning the inhabitants below to prepare for the approaching danger.

Castlesteads, about half a mile further east, is an elevated plateau of rock, having a sloping level surface of about half an acre, covered with bent and moss. On nearly every side it presents an escarpment of rock from three to fifteen feet high; along the top of this has been a rude wall or barricade of stone to serve partly as a defence against attack, or more likely as a fence to enfold horses and cattle. Within it on the south side are two oblong enclosures about twenty yards long by eight each, and on the north-west side is a large pile of stones as though it may have been a rude tower. This elevation is situated in a hollow and immediately all round it is an impassable plain of rocks and chasms. These are continued, more or less similar, for a mile or more on every side; so that this stronghold could only be gained by horses and cattle by circuitous windings, known only to those most familiar with the locality. In this place and others similar, then, in ages past, we may conclude that in times of invasion or when marauders ravaged the country, the inhabitants of Orton and Crosby would remove their cattle and other goods for security, which it certainly would afford, if such were to be had; first, from its secluded situation, for, unless previously known, it would escape discovery, and if known, a few men well armed and familiar with the crags would have baffled and perhaps overcome a whole army. Some authors suppose the word Castlesteads to be associated with Roman works, and possibly this place may have held out and been reduced by them. However this may have been, at no great distance to the north were found in April 1847 a beautiful silver brooch (Fibula Vestiaria) and a silver torque, in a crevice of the rock at a depth of about five feet. Possibly these may have been in the possession of some reckless Roman captain whose hardihood and reckless daring led him amongst the treacherous scars and hardy Britons, which when he discovered, in his haste to retreat flung away his cloak to free himself of its encumbrance, unmindful of its valuable ornaments.[5]

About a mile from Castlesteads, descending by a rocky ravine in an easterly direction, is a remarkable hollow called Sale Bottom, where are the remains of mounds and earthworks, to all appearance of a strategic character—perchance the battlefield on which the owners of the fold on Castlesteads have struggled to defend themselves and their property. It is a narrow area of level land, bounded on the north side by an escarpment of limestone more or less bold; on the opposite side is a more regular slope, while the ends are gorges more or less rocky. Across the level area of this bottom have been formed five or six embankments of earth and stones running from the rocks on one side and on the other ending in counter entrenchments, two of which, at about twenty-five yards apart, run parallel along the slope of the hill, and so defending the most approachable side. The entrenchment at the upper end has also a ditch on the outside and runs between the cliff in one ravine over a hill to another ravine. Scattered over this area are also seven or eight mounds, which lead us to suppose that after the action was over the dead were buried on the field. The principal mound is circular, nine yards in diameter; near it is another, forty yards long and about five broad. These are of earth and stones, and have been made of the materials forming one of the breastworks, parts of which are still left at each end; besides these, further up, are three irregular shaped ones, about ten yards long each by five; there are also three other smaller ones in different places, all within the area of the entrenchments. These mounds have never been opened, so that no idea can be formed of the people by whom they were formed. The word Sale is by some supposed to mean strife or battle, and possibly the various forms of Sel and Sill may be of similar derivation, for example, Sill How, near Odindale.

On the eastern slope of Sill How are the remains of raised banks of earth and stones running in different directions, apparently for a similar purpose to those in Sale Bottom—defence against the attacks of horsemen or chariots. Crowning the hill, not far from the stone circles is a mound which, on being opened, was found to contain in the centre a small chamber formed by four flat stones set edgewise, making a cavity about eighteen inches by ten and six deep; this contained a quantity of ashes and charred bones; over it was laid a rude limestone slab about three feet long by two. Upon this was loose earth and then another much larger stone.

Outside in the body of the mound were also found quantities of human bones and teeth and also the teeth of horses. Amongst the earthworks are one or two mounds, one of which contained human bones, miscellaneously thrown in at a slight depth. The south-west slope of the hill is called "Outliers Brow," on which, on making a road, a bronze spear-head was found.

In Stony Gill, near Winter Tarn, are also similar remains of irregular earthworks, running across a level piece of ground at different distances from one steep breast of rock to another, the scene of another of those struggles constantly occurring in savage ages. The most remarkable feature is a mound on the top of which has been erected a memorial or bauta-stone commemorative of victory. This has fallen from its erect position, and a portion of the top having broken off is still lying at no great distance. This again illustrates Ossian when commemorating a victory. He says:—"I took a stone from the stream amongst the song of bards, we raised the mould around the stone, and bade it speak to other years." Then contemplating of what would happen in after years he says:—"Prone from the stormy night the traveller shall lay him by thy side: the whistling moss shall sound in his dreams, the years that are past shall return. Battles rise before him. Blue-shielded kings descend to war. The darkened moon looks down from heaven on the troubled field. He shall burst with morning from his dreams and see the tombs of warriors round. He shall ask about the stones." But the time is now too far past; the chief is forgot—and who shall reply?

On the high ground east of Winter Tarn is a mound ten yards in diameter, near to which are some faint traces of an irregular oblong enclosure. Within this are two circles, respectively fifteen and eleven yards in diameter and three yards apart. The traces of these are very slight, as though a small trench had been made around some temporary camp. To the south-east of this, on what is called The Edge, is one of those large circular ramparts of earthwork; it is nearly obliterated by the plough, but seems to have been about fifty or sixty yards in diameter. There is another similar near Hard Ing, much more perfect, with a mound and ditch; some antiquarians attribute these to be the work of the Danes, as strongholds in their forays.

The last remains of a strategic character to be enumerated are on Bank Moor. Here there is a level plateau of land which has been fortified on the west and north by a deep ditch, formed along the brow of the hill. When the brow is a rocky crest no ditch is made, but it is continued across the north end to another breast of rock. This extends still higher, away at about an average of 150 yards, parallel to the other, to Raise How, a large mound at the southern extremity. The whole length of the plateau is about a quarter of a mile.

RELICS OF THE STONE AGE.

NEAR Winter Tarn at different times have been found various relics of the ancient Celts belonging to the Stone Age. Two stone celts, one of greenstone, the other of basalt. The one of basalt is broken and only a portion left; the other is perfect—with a hole in it to receive a shaft and be used as a mace or battle-axe. Another similar was found on Crosby Fell, near Hause Edge, but is now lost. One of another character was found in Threaplands Gill; it is of green slate, smoothly polished. This has been broken, the portion found is the narrow end. Its length would originally be about [ ] inches, having a sharp broad edge. Another, of basalt, was found near Gunnerskeld, of similar character, but more pointed at the narrow end. The use of these is doubtful; they are, however, though much larger, similar in shape to two others found near Winter Tarn, and these are almost exactly similar to such as are used by the North American Indians to strike off the skins of deer and other animals. They are used by placing the narrow end in the palm of the hand, and with the broad, sharp edge beat off the skin from the flesh; and undoubtedly those found in this neighbourhood have been used by the ancient inhabitants of Westmorland for a similar purpose.

In the neighbourhood of Winter Tarn at different times and at different places have been found three annulets, or as they are sometimes called, Druids' rings; they are all similar, being small flat circular stones of slate, and half an inch thick and an inch in diameter; there is a hole in the middle around which are concentric rings on the flat sides: they are also grooved round the edges.

A RETROSPECT

THE northern counties of England have, through all historic record, and in times previous from monumental evidence, been the scenes of constant struggles, sometimes between the different tribes of the inhabitants amongst themselves, or marauders; and at other times united as a people opposing the invasions of foreign aggressors, as the Romans, and after them the Scots, Picts, Angles, Saxons and Danes; each in their turn conquering in whole or part, and so settling as a separate people, or mingling with the previous inhabitants. How remote may have been the influx of our first colonists we have no clue; but ethnologists agree generally that these were the Hiberno-Celts, who came not later than four centuries before our era. These came in from the north, generally following and forming settlements along the hills and valleys. To them is attributed the erection of the stone circles and several of the mounds on our hilltops. As a natural consequence they were the first to give names to the various natural objects. These, as in every new country, are the hills, streams, valleys, and natural clearings in the forests, which they called by words synonymous in their language. To them belong such words as *knock*, (a hill). They, have, however, left but few names, being found more on the east and west fell sides.

The next race were the Cambro-Celts, who have come in from the south. These we trace in the name *Pen* (a hill) as Penhurrock, and the affix *Cum*, &c. Other tribes and people also mingled in the country from various sources, forming what were called at the time of the Roman invasion the Brigantes. During the Roman sway, which in the north was not more than 350 years, little change would take place in the real character of the inhabitants, as the Romans almost never intermixed with the native population. It was probably thinned of its inhabitants—not only from the draughting of young men for foreign service in the army, but more particularly from the fearful visitations of fire and sword on the revolting tribes, which was often the case with the Brigantes. The Roman era, was, however, a period of peace to the north compared with the succeeding 400 years, during which time it was subject to various invasions, first from the Picts and Scots, who ravaged the poor, helpless Britons, after the withdrawal of the Roman legions, for upwards of 150 years. Then came the Angles, who invaded from the east coast along the Roman roads. The Saxons followed, amongst whom there were constant wars. After them came the wildest and most erratic of all—the Danes. Under these Gothic tribes other words were introduced and affixes added to older names; villages and more permanent settlements began to be formed, requiring definite names: thus we have the affixes *ton* (Angle), *ham* (Saxon) and *by* (Danish), meaning a town or settlement. Thus each having a different language or dialect, words belonging to each have been blended into one forming the present Westmorland dialect; and so, as civilization advanced, and names were required, they have been bestowed by each different race and retained to the present day; and, what is a remarkable proof of the addition of names by different races, we often find two or three syllables in one name, each given by a different people, and yet each and all having the same meaning. The names now borne by fields have generally been applied to the same land for ages previous to its enclosure; and are consequently indicative of the existence of some particular race of people; or it may be some event. Others again bear peculiar names which they derive from some remains, even though these have been removed. These are often from mounds, as Affleber, a corruption from Anglebarrow; from earthworks, as Borwans, or from stone circles, as Stannerstones. Another curious fact is that many of these places where earthworks or mounds are or have been are said to be haunted. Such is the case near Reagill Grange, where a gate noiselessly is opened for the midnight passenger, and again as noiselessly closed. At other places a figure suddenly appears, passes by, and vanishes; sometimes a dog, swelling into an enormous size; again a calf or black swine, and not unfrequently a lady in white, whose antics are as various as her observers. This myth of the midnight air has often appeared to belated travellers, who, on daring her, have fallen victims to her fury. Major White of Reagill, one night coming through Blinbeck on horseback, saw something white in a tree, which he supposed to be a howlet. Having a gun with him, he fired at it. With this salute it began to swell and grew bigger till it took the form of a lady in white. She jumped on to the horse behind him, and galloped him through hedge, ditch and brake at a terrible speed. At last he landed home, his clothes torn to shreds, and his horse panting and white with foam. Another boggle haunts Langland's Geayte. This is supposed to be a Barghast from its peculiar *wawl* or *beal*. One old man tells the story that he was coming along on horseback with some sacks under him. On hearing the wawl he jumped off, and pulled off his sacks, thinking some one had put a cat in; he found none, but presently cats began to wawl on all sides of him. He then knew it was the Barghast, so mounting his horse he made all speed along the haunted lane. Another man walking in the same lane saw something black in the middle of the road; he, foolhardy, punched at it "an' wi' that it gev the awfullest beal. I tewk to my heels than, for I knew 'twas a Barghast." He told his tale to an old neighbour next morning, who replied "La, man' it'll be our cuddy, it niver come heayme yesterday neet," so off they went to see; and the cuddy it certainly had been. These appearances are often in the most lonely places, and in many instances the memory of some deed has in the ghost survived all remembrance of the action. Such is the case at Skellaw Quarry. Here a black man was seen to glide from point to point of the rock, and then mysteriously disappear, invariably at the same spot. It is a curious fact that there, a few years ago, some quarrymen came upon the skeletons of eleven human beings. These had been laid in an open channel or crevice formed in the rock, and then covered up. One of these had been highly jewelled, which bespoke considerable importance, having gold rings and bracelets on his fingers and wrists, and bronze earrings; the latter had discoloured the bones of the skull. The bones were carefully taken up, and devoutly interred in Morland churchyard. We do not know that the divine rites of the church were performed over them, but "The Black Man" has never more been seen. Along with the human bodies were also found the bones of the lower jaw and other parts of a swine, the provisions doubtless of the party who, whether explorers, merchants or hunters, have been fallen upon and murdered by some band of marauders; but at what period there is no means of ascertaining.

Between Reagill and Reagill Grange is a stone called "The Boggle Steayne;" it is haunted by a black swine, which crosses before the seer past the stone, and then vanishes in a deep pool of water. The stone is of immense size, but is half buried in the earth. Upon its upper surface is a natural mark resembling a footprint. This is said to have been left by the boggle. Another was formerly seen on the school, and another on the house between it and the stone; evident traces of some spirit of evil or perhaps of good, and who, like the Brownie of Bledwock

. . . . though lang sen geayne
The mark o' his foot's left on mony a steayne.

In following up the history of a people we find that each age had its characteristic superstitions, and supernatural appearances. The remote inhabitants believed in the transmigration of souls, and the return of the spirit to haunt its earthly tomb; these and the later Scandinavian races, imaginative to a high degree, and whose religion gave to every object and event a presiding spirit, have peopled our hills and bye-places with boggles, which for ages have kept in awe the minds of many successive generations. To such means, and the native wild and superstitious feelings descended from our forefathers, may we ascribe the belief in apparitions such as the reappearance of those dead, the lady in white, black swine, wraiths, &c. From the older religions we have the Barghast, the ghost of the tomb, whose unearthly lamentations warn mortals of fell mishaps, the Taisteral, a mischievous spirit of evil; the dobbies, brownies and fairies. In these mysterious spirits of the night do we trace the imaginings of a people long gone, whose works are almost lost; yet tradition has never failed to hand them down and down from father to son, yet each time ebbing weaker and weaker, till now the advance of the nineteenth century has marked the bounds "Thus far shall they go and no further"; now no longer the ingle newk resounds with the dread tales of a grandfather, and by the next generation all this will be forgot.

During the Roman sway Christianity was introduced into Britain, but it is highly probable that it took but little root in the North. The faint gleam of the true faith, if ever it existed, would be completely extinguished by the introduction of the Pagan creed of the Gothic nations, to the deities of which we are indebted for the names of the days of the week, and for several local names throughout the country. This wild religion, however, eventually gave way before the advance of Christianity, for about the year 630 when Edwin was king of Northumbria, the true light of the cross was first introduced into the north by Paulinus, who is said to have converted the Northumbrians. He probably followed the example of Augustine, who, to bring from the old idolatry and not to offend the feelings of the people, consecrated the heathen temples, and observed the heathen festivals; but dedicated to the observance of Christian saints. The next advance was to erect rallying places of truly Christian origin; these were crosses of wood or stone, which to this day remain in reality or in name in almost every village. One has been erected at Crosby by some devoted to the reformation of the people around, which would assemble the new converts to hear discourses on the blessings and comforts of the new religion. But this was not all straightforward. The country became subject to the incursions of the Danes, who brought back the old religion in its wildest and most erratic form. The infant Christianity fell before them, and Paganism was again in the ascendancy. Such, as its name implies, has been the case at Crosby Ravensworth. The Danes coming, find here a village with the cross planted on the green. They, without respect to rights of property or religion, throw down the cross, and hoist their standard "The Raven" symbolical of the mighty Odin, in its place.[6] The village, to its previous name of Crosby, receives the further appellation of Raven's-warth (the village or place) thus dedicating the valley to the presiding care of the Raven God. This, with Ravengill and Ravencrag in Crosby Gill, and the more direct name of Odin in Odindale, all indicate the ascendancy of that people who in their plundering inroads fought under the banner dedicated and sacred to the Warrior God. Christianity, however, again gleamed forth; the crosses were renewed and others erected. One has existed, erected on Maulds Meaburn green; the pedestal was found when the present school was built, and there is authentic record that it stood there in the reign of Queen Elizabeth. A curious custom at one time existed connected with these crosses. When a funeral procession passed, the corpse was lowered and the people, uncovered, sung a hymn; this custom is still remembered to have been observed in passing Meaburn by old people, though no vestige of the cross remained, neither did anyone know the origin of the observance,—an example of what we often find, a custom existing when its origin and the object of its observance is forgot. Another is also likely to have been on the hill bearing the significant name of Cross Bank, near Reagill Grange. Thus Christianity became firmly established, and wandering priests supported by the voluntary contributions of his hearers went from place to place, preaching the true faith, now holding forth from the steps of some cross, or with his hearers beneath some wooden shed which received the name of a church. A building of this character in all probability answered that purpose at Crosby for many years previous to the erection of the first stone structure. Churches were first built of stone about the end of the seventh century, when Theodore was Archbishop of Canterbury. He reformed the existing state of religion by having stationary priests supported by a fixed salary raised by a tax called "kirk scot" on all cultivated lands.[7] When the church at Crosby was first built of stone, we have no record.

The condition of the people up to the time of the Norman Conquest had made great advance since the first influx of the Saxons. A regular government prevailed, and permanent settlements had been made. Nearly all our villages may be traced back as having been first founded and named in those times, and even many of the single houses betray in the names a similar parentage. Cultivation was begun, and the land divided into hundreds, tithings and hides. The choice of boundaries is rather curious, and in some respects is proof of their antiquity. The first objects chosen, when convenient, are rivers or streams; the next landmarks are the wells and large boulders; of the former we have examples in Gunnerskeld, Rudkeld, Anna's Keld and Ned's Well, &c. Of the latter, in a district like this where large granite boulders are so plentiful, they have often been chosen, and in the old boundary rolls are called "Thunder Stones," the name by which granite boulders are known in the neighbourhood. Some of the more remarkable are the Cross Stone at Kiverriggs, where the parishes of Crosby, Shap and Morland join; the Stooping Stone on Harkeld is by some thought to have been a rocking stone; it is six feet high and lodged on a point of rock. It is mentioned as a boundary in a grant made by Thomas son of Gospatric of the manor of Hardendale to Byland Abbey.[8] Like all similar stones it is said to be haunted, and also has a remarkable propensity of turning once round every time it hears the cock crow! Another stone near Murber bears the name of "The Dead Man's Grave;" it is small and has two cavities in the top end, which gives it the resemblance of a skull.

The next objects chosen are the mounds or ancient burial places, and occasionally the stone circles. These were then regarded with a fear and sacred reverence which we might expect the common people of those times, young in the belief of Christianity, would have for the numerous monuments of their Pagan forefathers[9]; and it is quite probable that even then the same mode of burial might be adhered to; consequently these landmarks were as secure boundaries as either the wells or rivers. Another boundary often adopted in elevated lands is the watershedding line, or, according to the old wording, "where the water falling from Heaven runs both ways." As a proof of the antiquity of township boundaries it is worthy of remark that the manorial boundaries which were made soon after the Norman Conquest very frequently do not coincide, especially where the older boundaries have not been very definite.

MANOR OF CROSBY RAVENSWORTH.

THORPHINE DE ALVERSTEAN, son of Uctred, son of Gospatric, is the first lord of the manor of which there is any account. In 1140 he gave the church, with lands in the manor, to Whitby Abbey. He was succeeded by his son, Alan de Alverstean, who reclaimed the church, but afterwards, in 1174, confirmed all previous grants of his father. In 1218 Hugh de Hastings had a grant of free warren in Crosby and Tibbay; he held the manor under John de Veteripont, son of Robert. In 1221, Thomas de Hastings, grandson of Alan de Alverstean, confirmed all previous grants to Whitby Abbey. Also in 1243, this Thomas, who was brother of Nicholas, Lord of Alverstean, again confirmed all former grants.

He was succeeded by Thomas, his son, who freed the monks and their tenants from suit to his mill there, and gave them leave to grind their corn where they pleased. In 1265, William, son of Thomas de Hastings, confirmed all previous grants.

In 1313, Nicholas de Hastings, on the Inquisition post mortem of Robert de Clifford, held this manor, and Nateby, by homage and fealty, and 27s. 2d. cornage. The wardship whereof, when it should occur, was estimated at £40. In 1350, Ralph de Hastings held it in like manner, and in 1423 it was in the hands of Richard de Hastings by like cornage. In 1453 by a feodary it appears that Edward Hastings held Crosby by cornage of 13s. 7d. subject also to wardship, marriage, relief, and suit to the county court; and about the same time Lancelot Threlkeld seems to have held the same of the said Edward. From this time there are no more of the name of Hastings in connection with Crosby. The only relic of this family is a slab which was found in the churchyard, having an incised cross and shield upon it, bearing the arms of the Hastings; which differ from those of the Threlkelds only in colour. The principal residence of the Threlkeld family was at Threlkeld in Cumberland; but they had large possessions at Crosby long previous to this time, for in 1304 and 1320 Henry Threlkeld had a grant of free warren in Yanwath, Crosby, Tibbay, &c., and in 1404 occurs the name of William Threlkeld, Knight, of Crosby. Sir Lancelot Threlkeld, Knight, was the son of Sir Lancelot Threlkeld, by Margaret, daughter and heiress of Henry Bromflatt, Lord Vescy, and widow of John de Clifford. He was wont to say he had three noble houses; one at Crosby Ravensworth for pleasure, where he had a park full of deer; one at Yanwath for comfort and warmth, wherein to reside in winter; and one at Threlkeld, well stocked with tenants, to go with him to the wars. This Sir Lancelot has been buried in Crosby Church beneath the large tomb in the chapel belonging to Crosby Hall. The tomb is solid mason-work, ornamented with flutings on all sides, and on the south side with three blank shields, on which the armorial bearings would probably be painted. On the top is an immense polished limestone slab, without any ornament whatever; but on which it may have been the intention to have afterwards placed an effigy. Above this as a canopy is a low, flat arch, richly moulded, and on the north side enriched at each end with the arms of the Threlkelds, and in the centre the same impaling that of Bromflatt. At a later period the vault beneath was appropriated for the occupation of Robert Lowther, Esq., of Maulds Meaburn Hall, and probably at the same time the tombs underwent some alteration.

Sir Lancelot Threlkeld had three daughters, coheiresses; one was married to Thomas Dudley, Esq., who with her received Yanwath; the other two married two brothers, sons of Sir Christopher Pickering of Killington, Knight, by his wife Anne, who was daughter and sole heiress of Sir Christopher Moresby, Knight. One received with his wife the Threlkeld property; the other, James Pickering, and his wife Elizabeth, received Crosby. In 1527 this James Pickering held the manor of Henry, Earl of Cumberland, by cornage of 13s. 7d., owing also wardship, marriage, relief, and suit to the county court. He was succeeded by his son, William Pickering, Esq., who in 1532 was an arbitrator in a cause between Guy and Hugh Machell of Crackenthorpe. William was succeeded by his son Lancelot, who lived many years at the Hall. In 1568 he married a daughter of Thomas Blenkinsop of Helbeck; he had two sons, Thomas and James, and several daughters; who were married to different people in the parish, amongst others, some of the Thwaytes, at that time a numerous and respectable family in Crosby. James was bailiff of Crosby and lived at Craik Trees. He died in 1607. His father Lancelot died in 1603, and was succeeded by his eldest son Thomas. He, in the reign of James I sold the manor and part of the demesne to Sir John Lowther, Knight, of Lowther; and thus ended the dynasty of the Pickerings.

About this time there were considerable disputes between the lords of manors and tenants, the lords claiming an absolute estate in the tenements, and the tenants insisting upon an inheritance therein, according to the customs of the manor. The dispute between Sir J. Lowther and his tenants of Crosby Ravensworth was brought to issue in the High Court of Chancery, and a decree obtained in 1624; whereupon a grant was made to the tenants of all the lands upon payment of certain fines. This deed bears date 1629, but for eight years longer the fines remained unsettled. Sir John Lowther was at last compelled to agree and to confer to the tenants their estates to descend according to the common law, except that the eldest daughter or sister should inherit and not all; paying only two rents for a fine, reserving nevertheless the freehold estate therein, and suit of court and mill; but releasing to the tenants all services of ploughing, harrowing, shearing, raking, peat-leading,

&c. This dispute lasted about fifteen or sixteen years. Previously and about this time Sir John Lowther and also other lords sold many parcels of land totally free, reserving only the royalties and suit of mill after the twentieth moulter.

About the same time another dispute arose about the cornage, commonly called noutgeld, and serjeant oats or bailiff corn throughout the barony of Westmorland. In 1634 it was decreed that these duties were due to the Earl of Cumberland, and were to be paid according to the following agreement: the cornage was to be paid in money, and Sir John Lowther, escheator-general for the North, regulated the measure of oats. Instead of the old pecks containing eight and ten quarts being up-heaped, they were to pay thirteen quarts straked measure.[10] There is a list also of pout-hens collected by the land serjeant. These duties in Crosby parish were as follows:—Cornage: Crosby Ravensworth, 13s. 4d.; Maulds Meaburn, 20s. 2d.; Wickerslack, 2s. 6d. Serjeant oats: Crosby Ravensworth, 44 bushels 3 pecks; Maulds Meaburn, 70 bushels 1 peck. Pout hens: Crosby, 10; Gilts, 9; Harberwain, 6; Maulds Meaburn, 30; Odindale, 7; and Wickerslack, 8.

CROSBY HALL

PREVIOUS TO ITS BEING REBUILT.

Sir John Lowther gave the manor and estate of Crosby in marriage with his daughter Frances to John Dodsworth of Thornton Watlass, Yorkshire; he had issue John, who succeeded his father about 1659. This John Dodsworth had a son Robert,[11] who, it appears, though he lived at the Hall, or at least in the parish, did not succeed his father; for, according to Dr. Burn, John devised the estate to Francis Bayly in 1673, his faithful servant and steward, second son of Dr. Bayly of Penrith. He had issue Margaret Bayly, who was lady of the manor in 1696; and about the year 1700 she sold the whole manor and estate to the Worshipful Richard Lowther, Esq., of Maulds Meaburn Hall.

Black Dub, at the head of Crosby Gill, is the source of the Lyvennet, where, according to Dr. Burn, King Charles II., when he came in with the Scots in 1651, rested, dined, and drank of the water. This is authenticated by the Countess of Pembroke in her memoirs. The entry is that

"On August 8th, 1651, His Most Gracious Majesty King Charles II. with his army on his way from Scotland—passed Appleby about 7 miles to the West."

Tradition says that as they were passing over Crosby Fell a shepherd was met with. He was brought to the King, and questioned respecting the locality, and even acted as guide to the army over the moors. His name was Thwaytes, a family then numerous in Crosby. A rustic obelisk has been erected to commemorate the event, and a more vivid description of the place cannot be given than the following, extracted from a provincial paper published at the time.

"This place is one of the most solitary and dreary that can well be imagined, surrounded on all sides by an unenclosed heath; and, since the formation of the road over Shap Fells, seldom seen except by the shepherd or the sportsman. However, it must be recollected, that, though now so still and silent, it was once the great thoroughfare from Scotland through Lancashire, to the metropolis of England. To the solitary passer-by, who now can only hear the sighing of the breeze among the heather, or the bleating of a sheep, it may not be uninteresting to reflect on the noise and clamour that must have prevailed here on the day in question when the neighing of horses, the clang of arms and the shouting of men on a hasty march, (for Cromwell and his victorious army were not far behind), must have made a medley of sounds that can be better imagined than described."

On one side of the obelisk is the following inscription:—

HERE, AT BLACK DUB

THE SOURCE OF THE LYVENNET

CHARLES II

REGALED HIS ARMY ON THEIR MARCH

FROM SCOTLAND

AUGUST 8TH, A.D. 1651.

This obelisk was renewed in 1861 at the expense of Mr. Gibson, and besides the inscription on the lateral sides are bas-reliefs, on one side of a crown, for which Charles was ardently striving; on the other side is a lion, which unfortunately came in his way and overthrew his hopes at the battle of Worcester. It has been further commemorated in a poem, "The Lyvennet," by A. Whitehead, and also by Mr. T. Bland, who has sculptured "The Lyvennet Vase," on which the King, dismounted, is receiving a drink from the hands of the presiding goddess of the stream.

THE PARK.

THE Park at Crosby Ravensworth, of which Sir Lancelot Threlkeld boasted as affording him unbounded pleasure, lies to the south of Crosby, and is now known as Crosby Gill. It has originally been enclosed by a wall three yards in height, and of immense thickness; portions of this are still to be seen, the most perfect specimen being on the roadside from Crosby to Gilts. It has certainly been a chase of princely dimensions, containing within its bounds upwards of 700 acres, with a circumference of over six miles. The chase is of a very irregular and romantic character, being cut up into glens and ravines. A stream rising at King's Well runs the whole length down a beautiful yet wild valley, thickly covered with brushwood. This is joined in its course by three or four tributary streams. The Lyvennet from Black Dub runs down a deep and craggy glen, Raven Gill, down which the stream, after forming a succession of cascades, flows round the base of Raven Cragg, forming a deep pool called Aggy Lum; around which hangs a gloomy horror from the fact that it was once the scene of the last dreary plunge of a frail forsaken mother. Gilts beck, which gathers its waters from the bleak scars around Penhurrock, has also formed its course down a deep ravine. It is crossed, near Gilts, by a very picturesque bridge; the water runs through a cleft in the rock. This has been taken advantage of as an almost natural bridge. Its workmanship is attributed to Michael Scott, or, as some say, the Devil, who, flying over with a load of stones in his apron, the strings accidentally broke, and down fell the stones. He, unwilling to reload, but still wishful to turn them to some useful purpose, descended and formed the present bridge. On another occasion, however, he has not been so industriously inclined, for an immense heap of boulders near Wood Foot are also attributed to a similar accident; which he left in so careless a manner, as, according to the expression of an old farmer, "to spoil a lump of good land." A load these stones certainly have been, but more likely that of some antediluvian iceberg than that of his Satanic Majesty.[12]

The lodge, where probably resided the keepers, &c., is situated on an elevated part of the chase, commanding a view of the whole surrounding woods; it is now used as a farm-house, and has been rebuilt.

Many a time, doubtless, did the knight and his visitors at the Hall enjoy the excitement of the chase as the sound of hound and horn echoed among the dells.

These were jovial days at Crosby; but like their noble originators they are past and forgotten, except to the dreaming poet or the prosing antiquary, who have preserved for us something of the past in that fine old song:—

Oh those indeed were merry days
The merry days of old.

CROSBY RAVENSWORTH.

THE village of Crosby Ravensworth is remarkably picturesque, being situated near the junction of the stream from Odindale with the Lyvennet; these streams afford marked features of natural beauties, and are enhanced by the splendid sycamore trees in the neighbourhood of the Church and Hall. It is also a very good specimen of villages arranged under the feudal times, when the resident lord of the manor exercised an almost despotic sway over the tenants and other inhabitants. The Hall, therefore, as the manorial residence, would be a centre near which were the dwellings of the villagers. One series of buildings is known as Tenter Row; probably a corruption of The Enter Row, being at one entrance of the village, and thus called in contradistinction to Low Row at the other end. In these would live the tenants immediately dependent on the Hall, while others, not so closely connected, resided further up the village. There is the church also, impropriated to Whitby Abbey by one of the earliest manorial lords. It is dedicated, according to Randal Sanderson, to St. Lawrence; but Rev. Thomas Machell says it was dedicated to St. Leonard. This latter might originate from that hospital at York having lands here. There is a tradition of some religious buildings having existed on the north side of the churchyard, and a great portion of the land belonged; and from it must have originated the names of Monks' Barn, Monks' Bridge and Monks' Garth. Opposite the church is the vicarage, a truly characteristic building; it has undergone many alterations and additions under the late vicars, but is especially indebted to Rev. G. F. Weston, who has enlarged and laid out the grounds with admirable taste.

CROSBY RAVENSWORTH.

BATTLING TREE, MONKS' BRIDGE, VICARAGE AND SCHOOL.

There is the mill, where the tenants were required to grind their grain, subject to the lord's moultre. The inn, too, opposite the church, is a genuine specimen of a village alehouse, with its sign of "The Rising Sun," significant of the landlord's good ale, "always rising never to set," "cheering the heart it never saddens."

Up the village is a large spring; near it stood an ancient elm tree, about which the lazy wives of the village gathered in groups to gossip on the characters of their absent neighbours. The well still flows as usual, but the picturesque old tree is gone; its place is, however, occupied by a young one planted by Mr. Weston.

Another rendezvous of the fair sex was the Battling Tree on the Low Green; but those frequenting this were of a more thrifty class; for on the butt of the tree they were in the habit of battling or beating their homespun webs after immersing them in the water.

OLD HOUSE AT LOW ROW, CROSBY.

Near the Battling Tree are the Butts, where the young men were wont to practise archery and athletic games, such as running, wrestling, throwing geayvelock, &c. They consist of two mounds about 100 yards apart; upon these were erected temporary marks to shoot at. To the practice on these butts we may attribute the skill of the yeomanry as marksmen in times gone by. Every village green had its butts, and the villagers were required by the lord of the manor to practise, so that they might be able to contend with the Scots in case of an invasion, or border foray. In some places the mounds have been levelled away but the name still retained. They are to be found at Reagill near the school, and also at Maulds Meaburn. Time, however, has made great revolutions. These customs are now laid aside, being no longer required, and the houses in which the actors dwelt have undergone alterations more than once, especially Low Row, which was rebuilt in 1860, on the site of the old house seen in the sketch. The previous house bears the date of [ ] and was built by John Hall, a rather noteworthy character. When the building was in progress he was so struck with its symmetry that he kept stepping back and back, remarking at every step that it was "farther off an' finer"—"spacious and uniform," till he stepped backwards over into the beck; where, no doubt, his admiration was cooled.

During his life he made himself a monument, unknown to himself—which will bear his name, for centuries perhaps—by planting a clump of trees on an elevated piece of ground on Meaburn Moor; a landmark to all the north of Westmorland, and known to every one as "Johnny Haa' Trees."

CROSBY CHURCH.

ITS ARCHITECTURE, &C.

THE architecture of the Church may be best understood from the foregoing illustrations, which require little or no description. The Church was built after the usual cruciform plan, having a nave, chancel, transept, side aisles and tower. The first historic record concerning it is in the year 1140, when it was granted to Whitby Abbey. Previous to this time (if it existed) it would merely be a wooden structure, which would then be replaced by a stone one built after the later Norman style of architecture. Part of this original structure is still to be seen in the massive piers supporting the transept arches. Then again in the early part of the thirteenth century it has been partly pulled down and rebuilt in the early English style. Of this character are the columns and arches of the nave. Similar arches have also been erected upon the old piers in the transept. The change is very marked in one instance, where the arch is brought down and placed upon one of the old low columns, considerably to one side of the capital. At that time the Church would assume the character which it still in general retains. The richly moulded doorway belongs to this period, and also some of the windows, removed when last rebuilt, one of which is in the Churchyard wall. Towards the end of the same century the Decorated Style was introduced, to which the two north windows may be considered to belong. The next style introduced was the Perpendicular, which prevailed in the fifteenth century till near the Reformation. To this belongs the east window, which, from being badly proportioned and not in character with the rest of the architecture, is somewhat objectionable. To about the same period also belongs the architecture of the Threlkeld Arch and Chapel. The steeple window is another specimen of this style, but of a later period. There is a traditionary record that this tower was built about the same time as that of Shap Abbey, some time in the latter part of the reign of Henry VII.

The next most important change in its architectural history was in 1811. In this and the following year it was in a great measure rebuilt. The roof of the old church was leaded, and where the present new chancel arch is, near to the roof, were twelve small round-headed windows, representing numerically the twelve apostles; these were entirely removed. Most of the other windows were also taken out and replaced by the present ones, which are of a character that deservedly comes under the style The Debased. At this time the embattlements were removed from the tower, and some elaborate work introduced surmounted by pinnacles ornamented with crotchet work; many of the buttresses are also surmounted by similar ones. The porch and chancel doorway were ornamented with elaborately carved work, which though highly creditable to those engaged in the good work of remodelling the sacred edifice, are far from being in accordance with ecclesiastical architecture of the present day. The interior sittings, pulpit, &c., were refitted at the same time, and the interior decorated with texts from Scripture, scroll work, &c., chiefly done by George Gibson, Esq.

Another change in its history took place about 1849, when G. F. Weston was instituted vicar. He began by having the whitewash and plaster removed from all the columns and arches, which were re-hewn. At the expense of himself and friends he built the lofty chancel arch in place of what was before but temporary woodwork, and another arch between the north transept and the small chapel belonging to Crosby Hall. The sittings were rearranged and the handsome seats introduced in the choir. By the voluntary contribution of landowners, residents, &c., money was raised for erecting a vestry and heating the Church by the circulation of hot water; at which time the body of the Church was somewhat lowered, while the chancel was raised to its proper proportions. Previous to rebuilding in 1811, it was entered by a descent of three or four steps, and was then filled up.

The next objects demanding attention are the monuments. The oldest of these are the Threlkeld tomb and a small incised slab bearing the Hastings arms before noticed. These are in the small side chapel. There is also another, lately removed from the Churchyard into it, having an inscription of a Puritanical character; and from the half obliterated letters it has been to the memory of Ann Wharton, probably one of that family resident at Reagill Grange. Long ago a number of throughstones stood in front of the Church; but these were removed when it was rebuilt, and the stones used as flags, which, with their half obliterated inscriptions, may be seen in different parts of the Church. On one near the doorway may be seen an hour-glass and on another a small cross, and several others of individuals, who, although their names may be still engraven on stone, are themselves quite forgot.

Of modern monuments there is a large one in the south transept to the memory of George Gibson, Esq., of Crosby, erected by public subscription. It displays a good deal of artistic taste, having affixed to it three pieces of sculpture in marble, representing the figures Faith, Hope and Charity.

INTERIOR OF THE CHURCH SHOWING THE THRELKELD
TOMB.

The pulpit bears record to the memory of John Salkeld, Esq., of Meaburn Hill; it is tastefully designed in the early English style, and well executed. The stone is a beautiful sandstone, brought from Hause Quarry. The window and its masonry is the work of the Rev. G. F. Weston, in memory of Mary, his first wife. The architecture is very tasteful, and the colouring of the window rich—in the group, Christ receiving little children—are to be seen family likenesses.

The coloured window in the steeple was lately put up in memory of some of the Thwaytes family. A number of neat monuments have of late years been added to the Churchyard, chiefly introduced by the present vicar, to whom not only are the inhabitants indebted for the neatness and comfort of the sacred edifice, but for many material good works as well as spiritual benefits which he has done amongst them; and our earnest wish is that he may still be induced to dwell among us, and that he may long live to fulfil his parochial duties.

CROSBY HALL.

OF the architecture and character of the Hall little can be said, as it was almost wholly rebuilt about forty years ago. According to a manuscript history of Crosby written by Mr. George Gibson in 1801, he says:—"In the time of the Pickerings it is said to have been a building of stately dimensions in the form of a lofty tower; but this ancient fabric being suffered to decay was totally taken down and removed almost within memory," so that it may now be about 120 or 130 years ago. "The place was fortified with walls, ditches and ponds of water, and numbers of beautiful sycamores were planted all round." If this was the case, these trees must now be upwards of 260 years of age, and are, according to the same author, of the same age as those around Gaythorn Hall. Burn, in describing the Hall in his day, says:— "In the entrance tower are two windows, one above the other, of no mean workmanship; above the door are the letters I.D. for John Dodsworth, who repaired the tower, and cut those letters in the old work. There is a coat of arms, quarterly of eight, which seems to have been put up by the Pickerings." This is now above the door of the present house, and in the window above are some portions of stained glass with a coat of arms, Lowther impaling Fleming. A great portion of the moat is still to be seen; it encloses an area of an irregular oblong; the moat is supplied with water by a spring at the north corner. The entrance, a mantle tower and drawbridge were on the north side, next the Church, where the moat is now completely levelled up. Within this outer moat was another, immediately around the building, which is also still partly traceable.

Associated with the Hall is a curious legend which has been handed down in firm belief for two or three generations. The Hall was almost nightly visited by what was called a dobbie, a supernatural being which was no small terror to the inhabitants, and which made a great excitement in the village at the time. Various accounts are given of its form, sometimes a sheeted skeleton, sometimes a white bull, which was wont to lick the window-panes at night; it chiefly frequented the old tower, and when that was pulled down, it ceased its nightly walks; but not till it disclosed to the old man of the Hall the whereabouts of some hidden treasure, and also the exact time and manner of his death, which, it is affirmed, happened accordingly. Another account is that the old farmer had some hand in making away with the lawful heir, and as a consequence was haunted by the apparition. This version says nothing about the treasure; but his death was foretold, and when it happened the dobbie also departed. The story is well told by Mr. Whitehead, in his Westmorland Legends,—ending thus:—

Sometimes it lick'd the window pane,
In shap of a girt white bull;
Sometimes it shak'd the mantle tower,
Sometimes it towl'd the bell:

And thus it carried on for years,
To think on't maks yan whidder,
Till't auld man cock'd his teas—an' than
They beaythe went off togidder.

THE DOBBIE OF CROSBY HALL.

MANOR OF MAULDS MEABURN.

THE first historic record of Meaburn is in the reign of Henry II, at which time the Barony of Westmorland was in possession of the Morville family. Roger de Morvill had a son and heir, Hugh, and a daughter, Maude. This daughter was married to William de Veteripont, and carried with her in marriage to her husband part of the manor of Meaburn. This manor previously included both the Meaburns (sometimes spelt *Medburn* or *Mayburn*), and all the lands between, called Meaburn Field. The other portion of the manor belonged, in the right of succession, to Sir Hugh; he, being one of the four knights who assassinated Thomas a Becket, his lands were confiscated, and became the property of the King; whence the two divisions of Meaburn were afterwards known as *King's* Meaburn and Maud's or Maulds Meaburn. William de Veteripont then held the manor in right of his wife, and gave four oxgangs of land at Maulds Meaburn to the Hospital of St. Leonard at York. Ivo their son also gave lands to the same hospital, circumscribed by the following limits:—

"From the nether or lower head of Undercot gill, into the syke which is in the upper head, and so all along by the same sike southwards on to the ditch by the highway side which leads from Appleby to Tibbay, and so, nigh unto the public way or street westwards unto the boundary of Askeby, unto the mills, and unto the ground which the said Ivo had before given to aforesaid hospital."

Ivo de Veteripont was brother to Robert, to whom King John granted the confiscated lands of Sir Hugh de Morville, and made him Baron of Westmorland. Ivo was succeeded by his son Robert, who gave to the Abbey of Shap 22s. yearly, to be paid out of Maulds Meaburn in the name of alms corn. In 1243 Robert granted the manor to John le Fraunceys, son of Hugh, to hold to him and his heirs, rendering yearly for all services one pound of cumin.

This payment was to Ivo, but there were other services to be performed to the Barons of Westmorland, paramount lords of the fee. John le Fraunceys granted on the other hand that Johan, daughter of Ivo, should peaceably have and hold the several lands and tenements granted to her by her father, with the service of villans and bondsmen.

In 1257 Philip le Fraunceys had a grant of free warren in Westmorland and Cumberland. He had a son Gilbert, whose son Richard married a daughter of Sir Michael de Harclay, then the King's ward, about 1278.

In 1292 occurs the name of John Franceys of Cliburn, of an ancient family there, as a juror in a case at Appleby, and also in 1307; so that it is probable the family of Frauncis holding Meaburn, and holding and living at Cliburn were of the same stock. In 1315, at the death of Robert de Clifford, the inquisition finds that Richard de Frauncis held of him the manor of Meaburn Maud and Whale, by homage and fealty and the cornage of 33s. and the wardship, worth 40s. In 1342 Isabella de Vernon held Meaburn, the family of Frauncis having doubtless ended in a daughter married to Vernon. The name Richard de Vernon occurs as holding the manor in 1370, 1392 and also in 1423, including Whale, by cornage of 33s. In 1519 we find a Richard Vernon of Nether Haddon, Derby, holding lands in Newby and succeeded by a son George, doubtless of the same family. In 1553 we find Sir George Vernon, Knight, lord of the manor of Maulds Meaburn by the like previous services. He was succeeded by Sir Thomas Stanley, Knight, who sold it to Sir Richard Lowther, Knight, in the reign of Queen Elizabeth.

Sir Richard Lowther gave his tenants of Maulds Meaburn their choice to hold their tenancies after the customs of any one of a certain number of manors. They chose Ravenstonedale, then under Philip, Lord Wharton, and the copy of an indenture made between Philip, Lord Wharton, and his tenants in the 3rd and 4th of Philip and Mary and also in the 22nd of Elizabeth was to stand as an indenture between Richard Lowther and his tenants of Maulds Meaburn. Sir Richard Lowther, during his life, gave the manor to his eldest son, Christopher, and he also confirmed the indenture; but when he came into possession he was so heavy in his exaction of service from his tenants that they refused in many cases to comply, alleging that such was not the custom in Ravenstonedale, nor named in the indenture. The consequence was an appeal to some court of law.[13]

The land at that time was for the most part unenclosed, and was known as Oxgang, Demain and Improved Lands, or lands enclosed. The most important of the last were the Cow Pasture and the Ox Close; the latter had been enclosed sixty years previous to this period, and contained about 100 acres. The Cow Pasture, 250 acres; they were both used as common pasture. Another large enclosure was the Park, at that time fenced half way round with a wall of stone, and the other half with quickset hedge. Dryevers, Mires, Flass, Garth and others were enclosed about thirty years previously. For these improved lands the lord demands 12d. an acre and eight years fine; the tenants refuse, and it is proved that such were laid on in his father's time, and the Demain lands were raised 13s. 4d. in lieu. Then again he wishes the tenants of all lands that were Demain to pay eight years fine. In this he is defeated, it being ordered that they were to enjoy them for one year's fine, on account of having compounded with his father, and paying £500 and so having the customs alleviated.

According to the relation of John Lambe of Kirkby Stephen, aged ninety years, there were, when he lived at Maulds Meaburn, sixty years before, seventy-four oxgangs of land (the oxgang land was the greatest portion), and that then, and in the time of his father, the tenants paid 5s. for each oxgang as rent due to the lord yearly, paid at Pentecost and St. Martin's, and 7d. likewise as a mylne ferme, in respect of grinding corn; for this reason, their moulter was very light, only one peck of meal for ten bushels, and also the same for every ten bushels of shillings. The Demain lands also paid the same.

This Christopher denies, claims the 7d. as part of the rent, and that they ought to pay moulter after the rate his witnesses say is done in Ravenstonedale, namely, for all corn ground at the lord's mylne, except oats, they pay the 30th part of corn unground, and one 30th part in meal after being ground, and for shilling oats one 13th part for shilling and for making groats of the same one 30th part and for grinding the same into meal one 30th part. The tenants refuse, and the miller, at the command of Mr. Lowther, refuses to grind; so they carry to the neighbouring mills of Barnskew, Crosby, King's Meaburn and Rutter, at the same time saying they are not compelled to grind at his mill at any rate, except for a certain portion of land. This rouses his anger considerably, and he reminds his oxgang tenants that it is their duty to keep in repair the millstones, wheels, hopper, and race pertaining to the mill. The case was brought before the Queen's Counsellors at York, and it was ordered that suit be done to Mr. Lowther's mill only for 154 acres and 32 perches of the oxgang land; that for oats only are they bound to Mr. Lowther's mill; and for all other grain they can go where they will. This order is dated 31 Queen Eliz., 1589, and as affirmed, was publicly read to and served upon about thirty of the wayward tenants on Meaburn Green, hard by The Crosse thereupon; but they were either not there, or being a stubborn set, heeded it not; for Mr. Lowther's mill was still deserted; law was again referred to, and from the evidence given there were various infringements of the order; amongst the rest Thomas Kitchen of Wickerslack borrowed a peck of big of a neighbour, and got half of it ground at Crosby and the other half at Barnskew. However, to set all right a commission was ordered to set out the 154 acres, 32 perches. After much difficulty it was settled and a list drawn out of the occupiers, areas and names of the lands where each piece was situated. They are scattered all over the township, each tenant having a portion, and curiously enough the names are those retained by fields at the present day, with scarcely any alteration.

Mr. Lowther requires a general fine of one year's rent on the change of the lord, in lieu of which it is agreed: The tenants to pay 100 nobles on St. Peter's or Lammas next at the Feast of Pentecost, if Christopher Lowther and his brother Jerrard will be bound that it shall not be changed for eight years after October 11th, 1592. He next wishes to have imposed a running fine or gressome, which in Ravenstonedale is £12 15s. 5d., paid by a certain number of the ancient customary or oxgang tenants every seven years. The tenants of Oxgang land had to pay 25s. 8d. as boon rent yearly, and those of the Demain; after the rent they took their tenements with or without boon. The lord demandeth boon days over and beside, but in this case is defeated.

Another complaint is that the tenants do not comply with the following custom in Ravenstonedale, namely: If the lord or his officers cause a tree to be felled on any man's tenement, whoever gets the tree has to pay 2d. to the tenants, who also had the top, and was bound to fence up the gap or stoven till it was out of harm from cattle; if he neglected this, he had to pay 6d. to the lord for each stoven not fenced up. Also each tenant had to plant three ashes on his tenement each year, and two for every tree felled, for the increase of wood. Some of these demands, however, he could not succeed in having fulfilled.

Another grief is that the Demain tenants have unlawfully felled scores of ash trees in the park, and spoiled the coppice or young wood for spring. The tenants say it grew on part of their own tenements, and if they had gone beyond bounds, they had been cleared at the late court.

Another service disputed was the carrying of coals. The tenants of Maulds Meaburn had to carry sixty horseloads, every and each horseload containing two bushels after the measure used at the pit; they had to bring them from wherever Mr. Lowther chose to buy them, which was on Stanemore, and to carry them to his residence, which was at Lowther. They had to give notice to Mr. Lowther, each when he was going to bring his share, and Mr. Lowther was bound to pay the bringer the price he paid for them at the pit. Christopher complains that they do not bring their yearly suit, and are behindhand for the last year, twenty-five bushels. The tenants say he refused to pay them for the coals they brought. To remedy this Mr. Lowther has to pay for the coals at the pit first, which if not done, the tenants shall not be obliged to carry them.

Another grief is that Mr. Lowther had felled trees in the park, and wished the tenants to spring and fence; this they refused to do, and even pulled down the fences there were, and thus it remained for some time. It was finally concluded by a commission being sent to set out what ought to be springed. The first part was the lower part of the park, next the Lyvennet, which was to be cut and then well fenced for seven years. The next portion is the north part of the park, which was to be cut at the lord's pleasure, and then fenced as spring for seven years. The next was the south corner of the park, to be cut, also at the pleasure of the lord, and then fenced for seven years; but only one of the three parts to be fenced at one time, and at any time after these springs have had sixteen years growth. Mr. Lowther or his heirs may cut down the hazel and birks at twenty-one years growth, and the ashes at thirty years growth; it was also ordered that the tenants should fence the first, as their cattle were most likely to have the grass, Mr. Lowther being resident at a distance, but who was to fence the other two was not decided.

The fiercest squabble of all was the following. Christopher Lowther caused to be erected, as he and his witnesses affirm, a little court-house, on the middle of Meaburn Green; a number of workmen were at work upon it, and it was on the point of being finished, the frame and timber was set up; lathed and sparred, and thatched with straw on one side. At this time, being the 22nd October, 1585, a large number of the wives of the tenants, instigated by their better halves, abused the workpeople and Mr. Lowther, and even threw stones at them. This did not cause them to desist building, so on the night of the 28th, a number of the tenants, headed by James Fletcher, armed themselves with pitchforks, handsaws, axes, long-piked sticks, swords, daggers, and other unlawful engines, and levelled it to the ground. Mr. Lowther wished to have recompense for the timber destroyed, and the pullers-down punished. This trial is held at York, where the tenants and their wives had to appear in defence; in which they say that what Christopher affirms is all utterly untrue about their unruly conduct: that according to the indenture the lord could not build on the waste without general consent of the tenants; that if he was allowed to build this he would build others: they had spoken to him quietly, but he refused to listen, and so they pulled it down, for by so doing he was infringing upon the green within the town gates on which they grassed their horses for service upon the Borders; they say the house was a large one, intended for a court-house and for Mr. Lowther to put his horse in when he visited the town. A recompense of £8 seems to have been awarded him, and the pullers-down fined, some to £3 6s. 2d. and some to 40s. This does not satisfy, and he brings the trial on again, but does not seem to succeed, only in obtaining a decree to have a piece of waste ground on which to build a court-house.[14]

These disputes have been examined before commissioners who held courts at different places, some bearing date from Kirkby Stephen, Morland Church and Brougham Chapel; but when the cases were brought before the Queen's Counsellors, they are dated at "Eboracum."

The names of those called as witnesses give some light as to the residence of the neighbouring gentry, or those who lived in the manorial houses. At Reagill Grange lived Anthony Wharton, who some time was in tenure and occupation of Meaburn Mill. At Shap Abbey lived Richard Wharton, gent., who, as well as he at Reagill Grange, were members of the Wharton family to whom the lands of Shap Abbey were granted. At Little Strickland lived

John Rigg, Esq.; his father was steward of the manorial courts at Maulds Meaburn in Sir George Vernon's time. At Craik Trees lived Ambrose Lancaster, aged eighty years, and also Thomas Lancaster, both of whom were strenuous supporters of the lord of the manor. The disputes have evidently been very warmly contested by both parties, some of the cases standing on for five or six years. There are also accusations of base and wilful perjury. Whether the courts granted justice in every case or not, we know not; but the truth seems to have been often tampered with. At last Christopher Lowther, in summing up his griefs, concludes by praying to have an end of suits, and says he has been kept so for ten years by his tenants, that he has become impoverished, and having so many children he is utterly unable to do Her Highness' service upon the Borders, according as he is bound, as others of his calling. The tenants humbly reply that they too wish an end of suits; they too are impoverished; but that Mr. Lowther has always been plaintiff against them.

Another important service due to the lord, but about which they have not had dispute, was the Border service. When this service was required by the Prince, the lord's steward sent a letter to the bailiff and constables telling them what service was required, and with how many men. These they appoint and muster in great haste, some on horse and some on foot, according to their rate. Four men were also sworn to rate the charges for victuals and carriage in such journeys as going to the Borders required. This tax was levied only when summoned to go. Those who refused to go when warned were sent by the bailiff to the warden to receive what punishment he chose to inflict. In 1595 a list has been made out bearing the date February 19th of that year, of all men musterable in the Lordship of Maulds Meaburn for this service, of tenants and young men from sixteen to sixty years of age, levied by the constables, James Fletcher, Robert Atkinson, Anthony Wharton, Richard Hodgeson and John Winter, and Mr. Christopher Lowther, Esq., Landlorde of ye Lordship, and Leader of ye men; 39 on this list are entered as "archers furnished," each having to serve with "a nag;" one of these, it appears, is "deceased," two "under age," and three having substitutes entered as "his son."

The next list is "Tenants that are footmen" 59 in number, of whom 18 are archers furnished, 7 entered as archers, 2 as billmen, 16 not furnished, and 15 before whose names is the letter F. These were the fighting men, besides whom is a list of 28, who are "sons, and men not being tenants." From an abstract of the muster for Border service within the counties of Cumberland and Westmorland, taken in 1584, that of the two counties amounted to 8350, of whom Westmorland furnished 4142; 1400 of these were archers furnished, 1300 billmen furnished, 1342 able men unfurnished, and 100 light horsemen furnished amongst the gentlemen and their household servants.

The mustering places were Sandford Moor, where mustered 1981, Greenholme 2669, and Strickland Moor 1269. The last place was the rendezvous of the Maulds Meaburn tenants. There is still a lingering tradition of the last as a mustering place. In 1618 Mr. C. Lowther was in a special commission with Lord Wharton and Lord William Howard and others for repressing disorders on the Borders. When King James I came into England on his accession to the Crown, in 1603, he attended him with a gallant company from the Borders of Scotland to Newcastle, where the King conferred upon him the order of knighthood, and there is little doubt but that in that gallant company were some of the staunch yeomanry of Maulds Meaburn. In the list of names for those deputed to serve on the Borders are five Robinsons, five Parkins, five Winters, five Harrisons, four Teasdales, four Whartons, three Fletchers, two Salkelds, two Kitchens, &c. But by far the most numerous are the Addysons, who mustered 16; a name now quite extinct in the parish.

MAULDS MEABURN HALL.

THE Manor House of Maulds Meaburn originally stood on the site of the present Hall, but we have no record of any of the manorial families residing at it. The present Hall has been built at different times. The oldest portion is the north part of the body of the Hall. It has originally been nearly square, and lofty, somewhat in the character of a tower. This has been strongly built of hewn sandstone. This old portion may be traced by having around the bottom a champhered basement. This portion, has, however, been so much altered, re-roofed and built around, that it is difficult to form a correct idea of its original features. Afterwards the buildings have been extended; the south side has been partly pulled down and extended in that direction, forming an oblong, to the ends of which have been added wings. The south wing has two large rooms on the ground floor, one of which is wainscoted in the old Elizabethan style, and also one of the upper rooms; these are gained by a broad oaken staircase, which forms a projection on the west end of the wing. These rooms are lighted by large mullioned windows, and a tall projecting chimney gives a marked feature to the south front. A corresponding wing has been built at the other end, which projects beyond the north end of the old building. This has been used as a subordinate part of the house, in which were the wine-cellars, store-rooms, &c. At the same time also has been added to the north-west side of the old part a series of lower buildings, serving as kitchens, laundry, &c., and servants' rooms in general. Still later, the central part or large hall, between the old Hall and south wing has been pulled down, and again rebuilt in a mere vulgar and temporary style; at which time the present door and chief entrance has been made. Above it, in bas-relief, a date of 1610, but at some after time it has been changed; the 10 being made to represent 76, by incising a top to the 1, making it 7; and also a top to the 0, making it 6.

MEABURN HALL, SOUTH FRONT.

This date in its present form raises a query: Is it a doorway of the oldest part of the Hall, removed to its present position, and recording the date of its first erection? If so, it must have been built in Sir Christopher Lowther's time, three years after he came into possession of his father's estate. The date, however, is not very reliable, but it is very probable that it was built by his son, John Lowther, Esq., afterwards Sir John, upon whom, and his wife Ellinor, daughter of William Fleming, Esq., of Rydal, a settlement was made of the manor of Maulds Meaburn in 1615; and after coming into possession he purchased eight tenements, which make up the present demesne of Maulds Meaburn Hall; for in his time there was scarcely any left, the lands having been previously so parcelled out amongst the religious societies. Sir J. Lowther was one of the knights of the county in 21st James I, and also in three Parliaments in Charles I's reign. He bought the manor and part of the demesne of Crosby of Thomas Pickering, Esq., and then gave it in marriage with his daughter Frances to John Dodsworth. He also bought half of the demesne of Reagill. For his second son Christopher he bought the Whitehaven estates. This Christopher married a coheiress, daughter of Christopher Lancaster of Craik Trees, and by purchasing the interest of the other two sisters added the whole of the Lancaster property to the Lowthers of Whitehaven. Sir John died in 1637, and according to a memorandum extant, his widow lived afterwards at Maulds Meaburn Hall, where she died in 1659; and by her last will and testament left the sum of £35 to the poor of Maulds Meaburn. The returns of this not being used till 1687, the person on whose land it was, was required to make it up to £40, and pay 40s. yearly; which was done: from which time it was regularly divided up to 1770. The first few years there were between 20 and 30 recipients, but they have dwindled down to 15, 12, and as low as nine.

Sir John was succeeded in the estates by his eldest son, Sir John Lowther, who in 1640 was created a Baronet of Nova Scotia. He was a great sufferer for the royal cause in the reign of Charles I, and during the usurpation lived retired; but was one of the Knights for Westmorland in the Parliament which restored Charles II. His eldest son died during his father's life, so that he was succeeded in the family estate by his grandson, Sir John Lowther, who afterwards received the epithet of "The Rich." To his second son Richard he gave the manor of Maulds Meaburn. This Richard lived at Meaburn Hall, and was chosen Member for Appleby in 1688 and 1690. To him may we attribute the general enlargement and extension of the Hall, and the laying out of the grounds in the way in which they still remain. These improvements, to all appearance, correspond in character to about the time of the altered date— 1676.

At a short distance to the north of the Hall are a number of subordinate buildings, of barns, stables, &c., of more or less modern erection, the oldest of which is a well-built block on which is a square tablet having the initials R.L., Richard Lowther, and the date of their erection, 1693.

Another remarkable building stands near the road, known as Fletcher Hall; it is a lofty building, of about seven yards square, containing one lower room and one upper; it is entered by a door on the east side, and the lower room lighted by a window of three lights in the north; the upper story is lighted by two similar windows on the east side. Its use was probably as a residence for the stewards or managing bailiff of the lords of the manor, and from this has derived its name "The Fletcher" from families of that name. These have been an influential family in Meaburn for many generations. In 1618 we find record in the register of the death of James Fletcher of Meaburn Hall Fold, and there are Fletchers recorded so far back as 1588. The present Fletcher has been rebuilt at the same time that the buildings of the Hall were extended.

The grounds have been laid out in the then fashionable Elizabethan style, and tradition yet affirms that they were at one time the finest gardens in the north. The entrance from the road is by a doorway with cheeks of solid masonry surmounted by balls, and a court on each side, mantled with ivy. Within this is a large level area in front of the Hall, flanked on each side with a row of now ancient yews; passing to the left through another doorway we come to the south front. Here is another large open quadrangle, laid out as a bowling green with a raised terrace on three sides; at the south-east and south-west corners are two garden houses in which the players might regale themselves in the intervals of the play. Running between these is a row of yew overhanging the once gravelled esplanade, which is ascended from the green by a few ornamental steps. Along the lateral terraces were also at one time yews and spruces; the former are all gone, and the latter represented by a few remarkably tall and half-blasted trunks of spruces, towering far above the surrounding trees. To the south of the green is an area covered with a number of remarkably tall trees; this is surrounded by a high wall, alongside of which on the south side are a row of yews overshadowing what have once been neat walks. After making an angle, this wall, forming the western boundary of the grounds, runs direct to the north, where the road forms the boundary. The garden is entered from the field outside by three postern doors. Within the wall is a broad, raised terrace, running the whole length; ornamented with here and there a holly, yew or laburnum, all of which, like the other trees, have gained a large size. Along the north wall are also rows of yews, some of which have fallen victims to the axe.

In the back garden is a large well, walled around, five yards by three. This supplies a large stream which flows direct north; on the east bank is a row of yews, and on the other, laburnums, which in summer enliven with their gay flowers their dark and sombre neighbours. Overtopping these on each side is a row of gigantic Scotch firs, the largest in the surrounding district. The extensive area included in these grounds have been ornamented by walks and shrubs, the latter of various kinds, fantastically cut. The last which disappeared was two rows of box, forming a long walk amongst lawns or flower beds. All the different rows of yews, hollies, &c., have in the times of the Hall's splendour been trimmed and kept cut, and afterwards allowed to grow their own natural way, which in their present neglected state are perhaps finer than when they received the tender nursing care of the gardeners. All this was no doubt done by Richard Lowther, when wealth was pouring into the hands of the family, at a time when a princely residence was the great ambition of the nobility and gentry.

After these tasteful decorations of the residence followed the beautifying of the neighbourhood. The park was planted with the present trees, which though now few, are noble specimens of what were, in the memory of those still living, so close and thick and dark that no vegetation flourished beneath them. The thick forest of oaks in the Mains would also be planted, with the avenues of yews and holly. The oaks have disappeared, and a young spring has overgrown the whole. The most remarkable neighbouring feature is the avenue on Morland Bank. This is a long, elevated piece of land, stretching out into the low-lying holmes, and probably its name is a corruption of Mer—or Mireland, from the marshes around. This has been planted on each side with Scotch firs, forming an avenue of about a mile in length. The trees are traditionally said to have been brought from Lowther, and were, at the time of planting, a cart load each. From being so large when planted, they never attained so great a height. At the north end are Ratla Park and Hard Bank plantations, of about the same age. Of this we have a good guess: a man of the name of Wharton, who died about 55 years ago, aged 90, assisted in his youth to plant them; so that it will be about 130 years ago; while the yews and park at Meaburn Hall, if planted soon after the erection of the present Hall, may be about 180 or 190 years old. We are no doubt indebted also to Robert, afterwards Governor Lowther, son of Richard, who would follow in the footsteps of his father in beautifying the lovely valley, in which it was their lot to be placed. Nature had formed a district having great capabilities, and with all respect to the memories of those men, they have done their duty towards it with most praiseworthy taste, and what is chiefly to be regretted is, there are none to follow their footsteps, but "hewers of wood and drawers of water."

In the year 1700, Richard purchased Crosby Hall and the manor of Margaret Bayly. He married Barbara, daughter of Robert Pricket, Esq., of Wresal Castle, Yorkshire, and died about the year 1704. He was succeeded by his eldest son, Robert Lowther, who was sometime store-keeper of the Tower, and in 1716 was appointed Captain-General and Governor-Chief of Barbadoes. He married a lady by whom he became possessed of an extensive property in Barbadoes. She died, and it appears he returned to reside at Meaburn Hall, and brought with him a great quantity of sugar and rum, which was stored in the wine-cellar; and tradition still retains a vivid recollection of the superior quality of the Governor's rum. For his second wife he married Catherine, daughter of Sir Joseph Pennington, Baronet; and issue two sons and three daughters.

Robert Lowther, Esq., from his patrimony and landed property, no doubt was an influential man in the neighbourhood. According to a valuation made the year before his death, his property in Meaburn is valued at £105; the next highest is John Salkeld, £41; the whole valuation of the lordship being £698 10s. It was his intention to rebuild the Hall; with this in view he had plans made, and a new site chosen amongst the yew trees in the south-east corner of Stonycrofts, opposite the Mills. He had kilns erected for burning bricks in Eelmires, for that purpose, the remains of which may still be seen, and got so far as to pull down the middle part of the Hall; but his schemes were doomed never to be perfected, all further advance being stopped by his death, which took place in 1745. His death is said to have been caused by the Rebellion. The Lowthers were ever staunch Royalists, and either himself or his son James held out some favourable support to the encouragement of the Pretender; after whose misfortunes Robert, being of a very nervous and timorous disposition, became so perplexed and afraid of the consequences that it injured his health and was the cause of his death. He was buried beneath the Threlkelds' tomb in Crosby Church. He was succeeded by his eldest son James, afterwards known as Jammy Lowther.

This James, by the death of his father, by the death of Henry, Viscount Lowther, of Lowther, who died without issue, and by the death of Sir William Lowther, Bart., of Whitehaven,[15] who also died without issue, became possessed of the three great estates of Meaburn, Lowther and Whitehaven. James Lowther represented the counties of Cumberland and Westmorland for several years in Parliament, and was elevated to the peerage in 1784 by the titles of Baron Lowther of Lowther, Viscount Lowther, and Earl of Lonsdale; consequently he was the first Earl. He was born at Meaburn Hall, where he resided at different times while the Hall at Lowther was in ruins, being burnt down about 1720. There is every reason to believe Meaburn was his favourite residence, where he kept a large establishment, of which the dairy over the bridge bears unmistakeable evidence. He also stocked the park with deer; and there are many yet living who can remember the last of them being removed to Lowther.

RUINS OF LOWTHER HALL FROM A SKETCH BY LADY MARY LOWTHER.

In 1761 he married Lady Mary Stewart, daughter of John, Earl of Bute. Lady Mary appears to have been an accomplished lady, and extremely fond of sketching in water colours; some of her sketches are tolerably well executed. There is at Lowther a large portfolio containing numbers of her sketches, generally in the neighbourhood of Lowther, Ullswater, Shap and Meaburn; some of which are extremely interesting as depicting places now either gone or greatly changed.[16] He died in the year 1802, leaving no issue, and after his day, Meaburn Hall passed into the hands of farmers.

James Lowther was a man of noble qualities, but of very eccentric character, and many are the remarkable stories about himself and his spirit after death, yet lingering in the country.[17] One of the most noteworthy, illustrating his eccentric character, is that, on his once passing through the streets of London he saw a woman crying, with a child in her arms. His feelings being touched, he had enquiries made respecting her, and found her to be a handsome and beautiful woman, though of no high station; she had been seduced and deserted. He so much admired her that he induced her to become his mistress, and had her installed in one of his establishments. It so happened, when he was absent, she died; and for some time none of the household durst communicate the intelligence to him on his return. However, the body so much requiring burial, his favourite valet presumed to tell him; upon which he was immediately kicked out, and expelled his service. So great, however, was his affection for the deceased, that he had her embalmed, and put into a leaden coffin with a piece of glass over the face, and placed in his own private room. Two ladies' maids, who were attendant on her in life, Sir James brought to Meaburn Hall, where they lived for some time as sole mistresses of the establishment; and tradition still remembers their names as "Miss Francis" and "Miss Oliver."

Another character associated with the Hall, and almost as famous as his master in his own sphere, was Jos o' t' Ha', a sort of steward or bailiff for his lordship. He was a privileged favourite, and often used to drive his master over the moors to or from Lowther and Whitehaven; and sometimes, on the return journey, would indulge in John Barleycorn to a great extent. One story is told of one of these occasions, when he had imbibed too freely at Shap, in going past Scarr he saw some sheep in a young plantation cropping off the young shoots. Ever thinking of duty he drove them out, but soon discovered that two individuals put them in again. These he soon found out to be the Devil and Cross Jown, a notorious character, who had lived at Ploverigg, but was lately dead. Jos remarked that "as soon as he saw them he set off, and they efter him, lick for smack, over Harbyrn Rigg, an' they niver gained a yard on him till he gat to Howbeck Brigg, when he lost seet o' them." Sometimes he carried his drinking propensities so far as to become blue-devilled; in which state he was wont to whip them about in the stables, requesting any bystanders to turn the door. One old man who was called upon, did his work so badly that Jos cursed him for allowing to escape now a horned 'un and now a cowed 'un. The old man in despair replied "Let me dew ill or dew weel, I's always cursed."

Jos was one of those who had nothing to fear from the reproof of his master. A story is told of his lordship, who, to tease Jos, taunted him with allowing the old women and children to get sticks in the wood. "Lord, yer honour" says Jos, "If ye were at teay end an' me at tudder, an' the Divil etween us wi' a fiery stick, we couldn't aw turn them." But Jos was no neglecter of his master's property, as the following anecdote will tell. A neighbour of his being dead, the bearers were passing along past the court wall with the corpse, when crack went the report of a gun, and immediately Jos' broad face was seen above. "Oh Jos," said one of the attendants, "what for dud ye dew that? ye suddent shut at a corpse, man." "Dam the rascal" was his reply, "He's stown many a yat loop and crewk fra me; I was determined to give him a crack at last!"

Jammy Lowther was more famous after death than in life, for no sooner was he dead than his spirit, ranging about in the gloomy hours of night, caused quite an uproar in the country. At the Hall was heard his loud call and order, and his footsteps sounded in the rooms at midnight. At other times he rushed along the tops of the trees on Morland Bank, a headless driver driving his coach, drawn by six headless horses in a blaze of fire. Similar sights also occurred about Lowther and Whitehaven, and so great was the fear of him in the country that it was determined, with the assistance of a Roman Catholic priest, to lay his spirit.

The ceremony took place in Lowther Church at midnight, and so furious and boisterous was the spirit when called, that the priest, on coming to the words in the ceremony "forever and aye" was confounded by the spirit blustering, and calling "For a year and a day," "A year and a day," and he unconsciously said "For a year and a day." The spirit was content, and the terror of him somewhat abated; but at midnight after the appointed time, he again broke loose, and played his pranks with greater terror than ever. This could not be endured; a priest was again called, the ceremony again gone through, and Jammy Lowther's rebellious spirit was "forever and aye" conjured to abide beneath the frowning cliffs of Wallow Cragg.

Before closing the history of this interesting old place, there is a legend connected with it worthy of record. In what is called the Green Room, two brothers of the Lowther family disagreed on some family matters beyond reconciliation. As no agreement could be come to, neither being willing to succumb to the other, they parted and went abroad, with the mutual determination never to see each other again. Previous to leaving, the doors of this room were blocked up, and seals placed upon them, which of course none durst break; everything in the room being left just as it was when last occupied by the brothers.

The room was thus sealed up for many years. Part of the wax was to be seen on the door not many years ago, and tradition speaks of curious people going to the window of this mysterious room, through which were to be seen the chairs, tables, and open secretary, just as when left by the estranged brothers.

CRAIK TREES.

CRAIK TREES is one of the oldest buildings in the parish, having originally been of the class known as Tower Houses. The tower was at the south end, where the groundworks may be seen. It has been pulled down, and the material used in the farm buildings. In one of these is a small ogee tower window, and in the modern porch is a slab with rudely cut and almost obliterated arms of the Lancasters. There still remains in the interior the lower portion of a turnpike stair, by which the tower has been ascended.

It was a residence of the Lancaster family. The first of whom there is any record are Ambrose Lancaster and Thomas, aged respectively 80 and 52 years in 1591; they were sworn as witnesses in some law transactions between Christopher Lowther, Esq., and his tenants of Maulds Meaburn. Ambrose was the 6th son of Lancelot Lancaster, Esq., of Sockbridge. The next who is recorded is Christopher Lancaster, great-grandson of the before mentioned Lancelot; in him the male heirs of the family failed; he had four daughters, the first married to Sir Christopher Lowther of Whitehaven, who by paying out the other sisters, swept away the whole of the Lancaster property. Some of the Pickerings of Crosby afterwards resided at Craik Trees, but it is now in the hands of farmers. The name has originated from the cry of rooks; these are all gone, with the trees in which they must have built, with the exception of one ancient gnarled ash.

A little below is a spring of somewhat a sacred character, from which, in Catholic times, it is said water was taken to baptise infants in Crosby Church; it is now grown up, being a complete quagmire; but by thrusting a stick in, stones can be found at the bottom.

On Meaburn Hill is a large stone obelisk, erected by Thomas Bland of Reagill on the site of the house in which resided for many generations the ancestors of the celebrated Joseph Addison, whose father, Lancelot Addison, was born here. Lancelot Addison was the son of Lancelot Addison. He was educated at Queen's College, Oxford; and afterwards passed many years in travelling through Europe and Africa, and was known as an author on various subjects. He was afterwards Rector of Milston in Wilts, then Archdeacon of Coventry and Dean of Lichfield. He married for his first wife Jane, daughter of Nathaniel Gulston, Esq., and sister of Dr. Gulston, Bishop of Bristol; and had issue Joseph, his eldest; Gulston, Governor of Fort St. George; Lancelot, Fellow of Magdalen College, Oxford; and three daughters. For his second wife he married Dorothy, daughter of John Danvers, of Shakerston, Leicestershire. He died in 1703, aged 71. Joseph, his son, is well known in the periodical productions of *Tatler*, *Spectator*, and *Guardian*, and also from his tragedy of Cato, whose dying soliloquy is enough to immortalise any one author.

He was in succession Commissioner of Appeals, UnderSecretary of State, Secretary to Lord-Lieutenant of Ireland, and Keeper of the Records; Secretary to the Lords Justices, and finally one of His Majesty's principal Secretaries of State.

He died in 1719, aged 49 years. He left behind an only daughter by the Countess of Warwick, whom he married in 1716.

NOTE.—On the next page, viz.: page 79, there is a drawing of "Flass House, Maulds Meaburn, the seat of Wilkinson Dent, Esquire," giving a view of the house, with the gardens in front, and the Lyvennet in the foreground. This occupies the upper half of the page. The remainder has been kept for a description, but it has never been written.

GAYTHORN MANOR, ETC.

THE first record of Gaythorn Hall is that the whole, or part of it, belonged to the Hospital of St. Leonard at York. In 1281 they had a grant of free warren in Docker and Gaythorn. According to Burn it was next in possession of the Pickerings, and sold by Sir Christopher Pickering of Ormshead in the reign of James I. to Sir James Bellingham of Over Levens. This cannot have been the case, for in the reign of Henry VII., this manor, Levens, Helsington and Fawcett Forest were bought by Alan Bellingham, 8th son of Sir Robert Bellingham, Knight, of Burnshead. Alan was treasurer of Berwick, and deputy warden of the marches. He was succeeded by his son Thomas, who died previous to 1550. Thomas left two sons, Alan the elder, and Thomas, who married a daughter of Thomas Blenkinsop of Helbeck, Esq., and sister of the wife of Lancelot Pickering, Esq., of Crosby Hall. He resided at Gaythorn Hall.

After the Dissolution, the Bellinghams became possessed of the advowson of Crosby Church, and in 1597, Thomas Bellingham made a presentation of the living to William Willan. Gaythorn then passed to James Bellingham, Esq., of Helsington, eldest son of Thomas' elder brother Alan. James lived at Gaythorn as early as 1604, and it is believed he was the builder of the present Hall. He was knighted by King James I. at Durham on his first coming into England in 1603. He died in 1641. The property descended to his eldest son, Sir Henry Bellingham, baronet; he was knight of the shire in Charles I.'s reign. He was succeeded by his brother Alan, who represented the county in 1661 and died in 1672. Then followed James of Levens, his son, who died in 1680, and succeeded by his son Alan. He was knight of the shire in 1681 and 1685. Being a wild and gay young man, he consumed a vast estate, and sold Levens, Gaythorn, etc., to Col. James Graham, privy purse to James II.; who represented the county for many years, and left an only daughter, Katherine. She married Henry Bowes Howard, Earl of Berkshire. They had issue William, Viscount Andover; he died in the lifetime of his father, but left issue Henry Howard, Earl of Suffolk and Berkshire, in the descendants of whose family it still remains.

Gaythorn Hall is situated in a wild and dreary district, far away from any other habitation, and it is rather surprising to find so stylish a building in such an isolated situation. It is a large building, in the Elizabethan style, with large mullioned windows of six and eight lights each. There is a projection on the front side, supported by an arched doorway with three large mullioned windows in the upper story, and above the arch are the Bellingham arms. Within this is the door, above which is a rudely carved figure of a mermaid, and the footstones are curious grotesque heads. The lower rooms are large and spacious; the ceiling of one is beautifully ornamented with vine leaf and branch work, with the family arms in the centre. The upper rooms are also very spacious; in these are one or two very handsome stone chimneypieces. Behind the Hall was, at one time, the remains of a private chapel, but it is now all gone, and no record of it is left, excepting the upper part of a mullioned window, more ancient in style than the present Hall, which no doubt occupies the site of a previous building.

There is a curious legend connected with Gaythorn Hall, respecting a family who lived there. The husband was a Protestant, the wife a Roman Catholic. Their first born son the mother insisted should be reared according to her faith; the father objected, and wished him to be a Protestant. The mother, being a determined woman, insisted that if it might not be as she wished, the child should not be brought up to any religion. The consequence was, the heartless mother had the child put down into a cellar below the house, without any clothing. Into this place she threw it some straw and old rags to lie upon, and for its food, potato peelings, paste and dirty washings. These she threw in at a hole without even herself entering the place. Here the child remained unknown to any but themselves till it was six years old, when by accident a man about the building heard a peculiar cry. There being always curious suspicions respecting this child, he was induced to compel its mother to disclose its hiding-place, and it was brought forth, a hideous looking monster, unable to walk. The nails of its hands and feet were grown like eagles' claws, and its body was almost covered with hair, which was matted with dirt and filth. The child was then cleaned, clothed and properly fed, sent to school, and eventually, though enduring such hard treatment in infancy, grew up to manhood, occupied a respectable position in society, and lived to a good old age.

MANOR OF REAGILL.

—

THE first notice recorded of Reagill is that Maude, the sister of Hugh de Morville and wife of William de Veteripont, gave a ploughland of her demesne of Renegill in frank marriage with her daughter Christian to Robert son of Derman; which land was called Hynthornham. There is no land at the present day bearing such a name; but it may have been the lands now known as Thornbank, a number of fields lying near Hard Bank. She afterwards gave the whole vill of Renegill to her son Robert, he rendering to her for all service one hawk; which he was to hold of Ivo his brother. Ivo confirmed the same to Robert and his heirs in 1208. This Robert, in 1212, granted it with the appurtenances to the Abbey of Shap.

The next account met with is concerning the chapel of Reagill. The Abbot and convent of Whitby despatched a messenger to Rome to complain to the Pope that the Abbot and Convent of Heppe over-exacted their tithes of Renegill Chapel in the parish of Crosby Ravensworth. His Holiness appointed certain persons to examine into these grievances, and wrote in 1224 settling the matter thus: that the Abbot and Convent of Heppe were to pay to the Church at Crosseby in the name of tithes 6 skepfuls (*skeppas*) of merchantable oatmeal for the tithes of their land at Renegill (a skepful is a quarter), from land which is cultivated at their own expense, and by their own hands, at that time; but new land hence broken up, by whomsoever, not to pay. It was to be paid, 3 skepfuls at Martinmas and 3 at Easter; but if they let these lands out after improving, they had to pay to the full. Also it is lawful for the Convent of Heppe to celebrate divine service in the Chapel of Renegill, saving harmless the mother church of Crosseby Ravensworth, with regard to oblations, obventions, confessions, communions and burials. This is drawn up and settled at Gisburn on the 20th Kalends of May, in the year of Incarnation 1225.

There is nothing more respecting Reagill until after the dissolution of the monasteries, when the revenues of the Abbey of Shap were granted in 1545 to Thomas, Lord Wharton, who had been advanced to the dignity of Baron by Henry VIII., for the signal defeat which he gave the Scots at Sollom Moss in 1542. To him was granted the monasteries of Shap, Gisburn and Rival (Rievaulx) in Yorkshire, to hold of the King by the service of one 20th part of one knight's fee, and paying for the whole £41 11s. yearly, with the reversion and remainder thereof in the Crown. In 1612, King James, for the faithful services of Sir George Wharton and other considerations, granted also the remainder and reversion to Philip, Lord Wharton. The particulars of the former grant of Renegill were divers rents and services issuing out of divers lands and tenements, and all messuages, mills, tofts, cottages, lands, tenements, meadows, pastures and other hereditaments in the tenure and occupation of the tenants, amongst whose names are Winter, Blamire, Furness, Hugil, Addison, etc., to the number of 22. The descendants of some of these have lived in Reagill for several generations afterwards. The Abbey, after the Dissolution, was valued at £154 7s. 7½d. a year; and in the computation made by Henry VIII. is the following return of property in Reagill:—

Shappe nuper Monasteriu Com' Westm'

	£	s.	d.
Ranegill reddit' grang'	8	0	0
Ranegill firma vocat' Threplands	2	0	0
Ranegill liber' firm'		3	0
Ranegill lib' reddit' iij quart' lib' piperis			
Ranegill lib' redd' terr' etc.		13	6
Ranegill reddit' divers' bovat' terr' etc.	9	5	0
Barnskew redd' mol' aquat' blad'		13	0

REAGILL GRANGE.

THE ancient manor house of Reagill, or more properly the Grange, occupied nearly the same site as the present house, except that it has been a little more to the north, where, on excavating for the foundation of some outbuildings, were found various remains of groundworks and old floors. This position is immediately on the edge of a deep and rocky ravine, down which runs a stream.

On the opposite or north side of this stood the chapel, in a small field called Chapel Garth. Other fields near are still called Chapel Lands. Its site may still be seen as an irregular rectangle of about 22 yards by 6 or 8, formed by banks of earth, etc., on which are a number of large boulders; but it is nearly all covered with brushwood. This, after the Dissolution, would be pulled down, and the material used for building the present Grange. This manor being solely in the hands of the monastery of Shap, a lay brother would be located here as bailiff, (the lands above Grange are still known as the Bailiff lands), to collect and transfer in kind the different products of the manor to the Abbey. There are also traces of other branches of work having been carried on, for at the bottom of the field, in front of the Grange, were remains of tanpits, and some of the refuse. Other remains are also to be seen, to which we cannot now attribute any use, but it evidently seems to have been a place of active industry.

The manor house was at Barnskew, and what is called the Mill Road is still traceable from Grange past the Chapel through Byesteads and away by Hardbank to Barnskew. The mill is now quite gone, though the race is yet traceable, having fallen into disuse about 60 or 70 years ago. The present house bears the date 1676, being then in the possession of a family of the name of Holmes, whose descendants still reside there, but now as tenants of the Earl of Lonsdale.

REAGILL GRANGE.

Reagill Grange, after the Dissolution, became the property of the Whartons, and a branch of the family resided at it. According to the Register at Crosby, Anthony Wharton of Reagill Grange died in 1590; he was previously in the occupation of Meaburn Mill. In 1630 is another entry of the death of Mr. Thomas Wharton, an ancient gentleman. The next date we find connected with Reagill Grange is 1652; it is cut above a fireplace in an upstairs room, but whether it records the erection of the present building, its position renders somewhat doubtful.

The present Grange is one of those antique cross houses of Elizabethan style, massively built, with small, single mullioned windows, having dripstones above. Another feature peculiar to such houses is the stacks of tall, circular chimneys. On the north side is a small addition, up which winds the staircase; and on the south side is a picturesque porch, overshadowed by a gigantic sycamore, which might be almost coeval with the house itself.

According to tradition, the house when built was left unfinished, there being merely the shell without ceilings, and having unplastered walls, in which state some of the upper rooms remained till about 50 years ago. This was undoubtedly erected by the Wharton family. The Whartons (in what year there is no record), sold Reagill Grange and half the demesne to Dr. Lancelot Daws of Barton Kirk, and the other half to Sir John Lowther. Dr. L. Daws was educated at Queen's College, Oxford, and afterwards took the degree of Doctor of Divinity at one of the Scotch Universities. He was instituted vicar of Barton in 1608. He was also rector of Asby, instituted in 1618. He was likewise prebendary of Carlisle, and, according to Dr. Burn, died in 1653; so that the date, 1652, for the erection of the Grange, is somewhat questionable, if built by the Whartons.

PLEASURE GROUNDS AT REAGILL

LAID OUT BY THOMAS BLAND.

But the vicissitudes of life and fortune are sometimes curious. It is well known that the Wharton property "never did any luck," and it is quite possible Reagill Grange had to be sold under some strain as soon as built, and it might be purchased by Dr. Daws just before he died. It remained in the possession of this family up to 1700, at which time an addition has been made to the north side, where there is a lintel of a doorway bearing that date, with the initials T & E D., with a bird, partly intended as heraldic. This must have therefore been done by Thomas Daws, nephew of Lancelot. Soon after this, the Grange, with the remaining half of the demesne, was sold to Sir John Lowther, to whose descendants it now belongs, and has ever since been in the occupation of the Thwaytes family as tenants.

(HERE THE TEXT ENDS).

[The view of the pleasure ground, no description of which was written, is taken about half way from the entrance. The recumbent figure on the right is Venus, which, with the lion, is now almost hidden by bushes. Beyond was the "Shakespeare corner," with scenes from his plays; facing the reader stands Sir Walter Scott, and below him three bas-reliefs illustrating his characters. The paintings are gone, and the arch is covered with a mass of ivy; it will be seen that one was mounted even in the wall of the farm house.

To the left is a corner of the terrace, beyond which the lower lawn continues between the two great vases. The panel below and to the left of the further vase represents Science trimming the lamp of Life.

The grounds fall far short of their former glory: only an artist could have kept them what they were; but though it misses "the touch of a vanished hand," the quiet garden is still a place of great interest and beauty.]

FOOTNOTES:

[1] The route by Overborough, Borough Bridge and Kirkby Thore was the Maiden Way; but it is probable that Agricola's first advance to this district was made along the coast.

[2] For full details of the most recent excavations and finds, with plans, see reports on "A Romano-British settlement at Ewe Close, Crosby Ravensworth," by W. G. Collingwood, F.S.A., (1907-8) *Transactions*, Cumberland and Westmorland Antiquarian and Archæological Society, N.S., vols. viii. and ix.

[3] The exact wording is:--"Near the head of which (the Lowther) is a well which, like Euripus, ebbs and flows several times in a day," a much less remarkable thing. Apparently Mr. Bland's informant has misquoted in conversation. The second edition of Camden's _Britannia_ (1723) comments that this phenomenon is not infrequent in rocky country, and not usually lasting; and that there was then no ebbing fountain to be heard of near Shap.

[4] This idea is that of Stukeley; it had, at the time, a very large following, but is now rejected.

[5] More probably both are pre-Roman. They are now in the Museum of the Society of Antiquaries.

[6] Canon Weston gave as a possible meaning of the puzzling word Ravensworth, "Hill of the Standard of the Raven," with the reservation that this failed if the Danes did not reach here. Others think the name is corrupted from Ravensthwaite, Raven's clearing. But far more interesting than the meaning is the pains with which the author traces out the historical steps by which the name, as he understands it, was built up.

[7] According to Stubbs, the belief that Theodore was the founder of the parochial system is mistaken; but his legislation aided its development.

[8] The authority for this sentence is not clear, as the charter granting Hardendale to Byland Abbey is not forthcoming. Perhaps Mr. Bland has been misinformed by some one who had read the charter of Thomas son of Gospatric granting to Shap Abbey the land on which the abbey stood; here a "great stone" is mentioned, but this is between Raset and the Lowther, quite a different spot. Mr. Bland is certainly not responsible for the confusion.

[9] Prof. Boyd Dawkins relates a remarkable instance of this feeling within living memory. About 1859 a Manx farmer offered up a calf as a burnt

sacrifice, to appease the spirits of the tumuli, disturbed by archæological spade-work!

[10] Straked, levelled off at the top, as opposed to heaped measure.

[11] There must be a mistake here, for if this Robert had been a descendant in any degree of John and Frances, he would have succeeded to Thornton Watlass, and lived there. As a matter of fact, the estate went to John's next brother, whose descendants have it still. John Dodsworth was never more than heir apparent; according to the Visitation of Yorkshire in 1665, he was dead, his father was seventy years of age, and he and Frances had had two children, Helen, who died young, and John, then aged sixteen. Hence, when the latter died, his son, if he had one, would be in the direct line of descent. Perhaps Robert was a servant, and had adopted his master's name; as was sometimes done in olden times.

[12] It has been remarked that in England anything ancient is attributed to one of four authors—Julius Cæsar, King Arthur, the Druids or the Devil. Julius Cæsar did not reach the north, and Michael Scott fills his place.

[13] It seems that the documents from which Mr. Bland gathered these curious particulars, represent the defendants', that is the tenants', side of the question; and it is very hard to tell whether the oppression they allege was real or imaginary. On the other hand, Mr. Lowther undoubtedly had cause for complaint, for on Mr. Bland's showing, the tenants more than once did wilful damage, and refused to comply with the order of the court.

A possible explanation is this: the Vernons were absentee landlords, and left things to take care of themselves; Sir Richard Lowther expected things to be managed properly, and saw that they were; and the change would not be popular, though perfectly just and fair. Something about the story suggests that the trouble was organised by some individual who possessed professional knowledge; perhaps the former steward had been dismissed by Sir Richard, and was taking his revenge in this way.

[14] We are inclined to think that this result, which Mr. Bland rates rather low, constituted a decisive success. The court had already shown that the tenants' method of redress was unlawful, had punished them for it, and made them pay compensation for the damage they had done. It might be argued at this point that they had a genuine grievance, and were merely wrong in their choice of remedy; but the decree deprives them of this excuse; for the court would not have permitted Mr. Lowther to have a piece of waste land for this purpose, if by building there he would be infringing the rights of the tenants. Hence his position is justified from the very beginning.

[15] The owner of Whitehaven was Sir James, his father's second cousin, son of Sir John, the great maker of the town. Sir William Lowther was his fourth

cousin, and left him Marske. Lowther came to him from his second cousin. His eventual heir, Sir William Lowther, was the son of his third cousin; the latter also inherited the title of Viscount Lonsdale under a special and remarkable limitation; this had been conferred on "Sir Jammy" when it was seen that his earldom was going to die out. The new peer was created Earl of Lonsdale in 1807; it was reported in 1828, correctly or otherwise, that he had the offer of a dukedom.

[16] A sketch of Shap Stones, made by her in 1775, is reproduced in Cumberland and Westmorland Antiquarian and Archæological Society's *Transactions*, vol. xv., article 4.

[17] Few men have been more bitterly attacked than James Lowther has been, both during his life, and after his death. He was masterful and capricious, a combination of qualities which does not make for popularity; he was devoted to electioneering, which earned him enemies; and it is worth noting that his chief detractors have a distinct political bias. They include Horace Walpole; Boswell, whose Parliamentary ambitions he disappointed, and above all, Rev. Alex. Carlyle, who devotes a page of his memoirs to a compilation of the worst epithets and opinions permissible to a Doctor of Divinity. Some of this is quoted in the *Dictionary of National Biography* article, omitting, however, the fact that the passage begins by showing the writer's sympathy with his great rival, the Duke of Portland.

Sir James was a benefactor to the town of Whitehaven, and it was he who secured the first return to Parliament of the younger Pitt—from Appleby. An amusing tale is told of him that he once fought a duel with a learned serjeant-at-law, who had made free with his character in a case. At the meeting, the learned serjeant is said to have shot his own toe! It is hard to believe that he would have been called "Sir Jammy" till his death, though he had long been a peer, had he really been "more detested than any man living" as Carlyle asserts he was; or the suggestion that he was a tyrant over his dependents and tenants in view of the fact that his funeral, which was, by his direction, strictly private and unannounced, "a large crowd of people from the neighbourhood were assembled, and behaved with the greatest respect, decency and decorum," as the *Gentleman's Magazine* quaintly puts it.

Milton Keynes UK
Ingram Content Group UK Ltd.
UKHW030743071024
449371UK00006B/606